SCRIBBLING THE CAT

ALEXANDRA FULLER was born in England in 1969 and in 1972 she moved with her family to a farm in what was then Rhodesia. After that country's civil war in 1981, the Fullers moved first to Malawi, then to Zambia. Fuller now lives in Wyoming and has two children.

ALSO BY ALEXANDRA FULLER

Don't Let's Go to the Dogs Tonight:

An African Childhood

ALEXANDRA FULLER

SCRIBBLING THE CAT

TRAVELS WITH AN AFRICAN SOLDIER

PICADOR

First published 2004 by The Penguin Press,
a member of Penguin Group (USA) Inc., New York

This edition published 2005 by Picador
an imprint of Pan Macmillan Ltd
Pan Macmillan, 20 New Wharf Road, London N1 9RR
Basingstoke and Oxford
Associated companies throughout the world
www.panmacmillan.com

ISBN 0 330 43399 7

Grateful acknowledgement is made for permission to reprint excerpts
from *Echoing Silences* by Alexander Kanengoni, Baobab Books, Zimbabwe, 1997.
Reprinted by permission of the publisher.

The author would like to acknowledge Peter Godwin and Ian Hancock,
the authors of *Rhodesians Never Die: The Impact of War and Political Change
on White Rhodesia, c. 1970–1980* and would also like to give special thanks
to Sean Jacobs, Jessica Blatt and Oliver Payne.

1 3 5 7 9 8 6 4 2

A CIP catalogue record for this book is available from
the British Library.

Printed and bound in Great Britain by
Mackays of Chatham plc, Chatham, Kent

This is a true story about a man and about the journey that I took with that man. It is a story about the continuing relationship that grew between the man and me and it is a story about the land over which we journeyed. But it is only my story; a slither of a slither of a much greater story. It is not supposed to be an historic document of fact.

Even if you were to do as I did—leave your family and your real, routine-fat life and follow a feeling in your gut that tells you to head south and east with a man who has a reputation for Godliness and violence—you will not find the man whom I call K. You will not find where he lives. You will not be able to trace our steps.

I have covered our tracks as a good soldier always does.

But, as a fallen soldier might, I have broken the old covenant, "What goes on tour, stays on tour."

Because what is important isn't K himself, or me myself, or Mapenga and St. Medard and the whole chaotic, poetic mess of people that turned this journey of curiosity into an exploration of life and death and the fear of living and dying and the difficulty of separating love and judgment from passion and duty.

What is important is the story.

Because when we are all dust and teeth and kicked-up bits of skin—when we're dancing with our own skeletons—our words might be all that's left of us.

Sole restaurant

PART ONE

Sole Valley, Zambia

So when he finally heard the section commander talking about civilizations that existed in the country before the coming of the white man, he was shocked to discover the history of his people did not start with the coming of the whites. The section commander began with Munhumutapa and the Rozvi empires during the Great Zimbabwe civilization, and continued on to the coming of the white man and the first chimurenga, and on through the various forms of colonial government up to Ian Smith's UDI, when the last bridge between blacks and whites was burned down and the only way left to communicate was through violence: the war, the second chimurenga.

➤ From *Echoing Silences* by Alexander Kanengoni

Uncharacteristic Sole Flood

Road sign, Zambia

BECAUSE IT IS THE LAND that grew me, and because they are my people, I sometimes forget to be astonished by Africans.

But I was astonished, almost to death, when I met K.

For a start, K was not what I expected to see here.

Not here, where the elevation rises just a few feet above ennui and where even the Goba people—the people who are *indigenous* to this area—look displaced by their own homes, like refugees who are trying to flee their place of refuge. And where the Tonga people—the nation that was shifted here in the 1950s, when the colonial government flooded them out of their ancestral valley to create Lake Kariwa—look unrequitedly vengeful and correspondingly despondent. And where everyone else looks like a refugee worker; sweat-drained, drunk, malarial, hungover, tragic, recently assaulted.

Down here, even those who don't go *looking* for trouble are scarred from the accidents of Life that stagger the otherwise uninterrupted tedium of heat and low-grade fever: boils, guns, bandit attacks, crocodiles, insect bites. No ripped edge of skin seems to close properly in this climate. Babies die too young and with unseemly haste.

If you count my parents and K, there are perhaps a wrecked village's worth of scattered people—out of a total population of about sixty thousand—who have voluntarily moved to the Sole Valley from elsewhere. That's if you *don't* count the occasional, evaporating aid workers who slog out this far from hope and try to prevent the villagers from losing their lives with such apparent carelessness. And if you don't count the Italian nuns at the mission hospital who are here as the result of a *calling* from God (more like an urgent shriek, I have no doubt).

Sole Valley is a V-shaped slot of goat-dusted scrub between the Chabija and Pepani Rivers in eastern Zambia. The town of Sole has metastasized off the cluster of buildings that make up the border post between Zambia and Zimbabwe. It consists of customs and immigration buildings, a (new and very smart) police station, an enormous tarmac parking lot for trucks, and a series of shabby tin and reed shacks that billow tarpaulins or plastic sheeting in a feeble protest against rain or dust and that offer for sale black market sugar, cooking oil, salt, mealie meal, and bread.

WELCOME TO SOLE, says the sign. SPEED KILLS, CONDOMS SAVE.

People at the border post climb out of their cars and you see them looking around and you can hear them thinking, Save me from what?

Guinea fowl destined for a torturous journey into someone's pot clatter from their bush-tambo baskets, "Nkanga, nkanga!" and the Heuglin's robins call from the dust-coated shrubs, "It's-up-to-you, it's-up-to-you, up-to-you, UP-TO-YOU."

Truck drivers in diesel-stained undershirts slouch in the shade of brothels and taverns, suffocating their boredom with women, beer, and cigarettes. A sign dangling above the shelves of one tavern, whose wares include not only beer and cigarettes but also condoms and headache pills, asks, HAVE YOU COME TO SOLVE MY PROBLEMS OR TO MULTIPLY THEM? Prostitutes lounge from trucker to trucker, casually soliciting in a hip-sliding sly way that hides their urgency. It's a deadly business. Cutthroat and throat-cut. Girls as young as twelve will sell themselves to the long-haul truckers for as little as a meal or a bar of soap.

In the shade of a shack that advertises MAX BARBERS ARC WELDING AND BATTERY CHARGE NOW OPEN, a truck yawns and surveys its parts, which are vomited greasily on the ribbed earth in front of it, while a young man in a shiny nylon soccer shirt has his hair braided into porcupine spikes by a woman with deft fingers.

And next to a sign that says RELAX & DISCUS RESTARUNT WE SALE SHIMA & TEA, two women from the Watchtower Society sit out in the sun with their legs stretched out in front of them, stern in their reproachfully white robes. They drink Coke and eat cakes of fried mealie meal.

There are, in Africa, many more glamorous and inhabitable addresses than this low sink of land on the edge of perpetual malaria. Scratch the surface of anyone who has voluntarily come to this place—and who is unguardedly drunk at the time—and you will invariably uncork a wellspring of sorrow or a series of supremely unfortunate events and, very often, both.

Scratch-and-sniff.

Stiff upper lips crack at the edge of the bar, and tears spill and waves of unaccustomed emotion swallow whole brandy-and-Coke-smelling days. These tidal waves of sadness and hopeless nostalgia (not the hankering for a happy, irretrievable past, but the much worse sensation of regret for a past that is unbearably sad and irrevocably damaged) are more prevalent when the heat gets too much or when Christmas creeps around and soaks the senses with the memory of all that was once promising and hopeful about life. And then tight tongues grow soft with drink and the unavoidable sadness of the human condition is debated in ever decreasing circles until it sits on the shoulders of each individual in an agonizingly concentrated lump. Eventually someone drinks himself sober and declares that life is short and vicious and unveeringly cruel, and perhaps it's best not to talk about it.

The hangovers from these drunken confessions of titanic misery (aborted marriages, damaging madness, dead children, lost wars, unmade fortunes) last nine or ten months, during which time no one really talks about *anything*, until the pressure of all the unhappiness builds up again to breaking point and there is another storm of heartbreaking confessions.

But K, perfectly sober and in the bright light of morning, *volunteered* his demons to me, almost immediately. He hoisted them up for my inspection, like gargoyles grinning and leering from the edge of a row of pillars. And I was too curious—too amazed—to look the other way.

It bloody nearly killed me.

THE YEAR THAT I went home from Wyoming to Zambia for Christmas—the year I met K—it had been widely reported by the international press that there was a drought in the whole region. A drought that had started by eating the crops in Malawi and Zimbabwe and had gone on to inhale anything edible in Zambia and Mozambique. It was a drought that didn't stop gorging until it fell into the sea, bloated with the dust of a good chunk of the lower half of Africa's belly.

News teams from all around the world came to take pictures of starving Africans and in the whole of central and southern Africa they couldn't find people more conveniently desperate— by which I mean desperate *and* close to both an international airport and a five-star hotel—than the villagers who live here. So they came with their cameras and their flak jackets and their little plastic bottles of hand sanitizer and took pictures of these villagers who were (as far as the villagers themselves were concerned) having an unusually fat year on account of unexpected and inexplicably generous local rain and the sudden, miraculous arrival of bags and bags of free food, which (in truth) they could use every year, not only when the rest of Africa suffered.

The television producers had to ask the locals—unused to international attention—to stop dancing and ululating in front of the camera. Couldn't they try to look subdued?

"Step away from the puddles."

Rain slashed down and filming had to stop. The sun came out and the world steamed a virile, exuberant green. The Sole Valley looked disobediently—at least from the glossy distance of videotape—like the Okavango Swamps. Women and children gleamed. Goats threatened to burst their skins. Even the donkeys managed to look fortunate and plump. In a place where it is dry for nine months at a stretch, even the slightest breath of rain can be landscape-altering and can briefly transform the people into an impression of tolerable health.

"Explain to them that this is *for their own good.* God knows, I am not doing this for *my* entertainment."

If the television crews had wanted misery, they had only to walk a few meters off the road and into the nearest huts, where men, women, and children hang like damp chickens over long drops losing their lives through their frothing bowels. But HIV/ AIDS is its own separate documentary.

Life expectancy in this dry basin of land has just been offi-cially reduced to thirty-three. How do you film an absence? How do you express in pictures the disappearance of almost everyone over the age of forty?

"Please ask those young boys to look hungry."

The young boys obligingly thrust their hips at the camera and waggled pink tongues at the director.

Sole Valley children

Characteristic Malidadi Flood

Mum and dogs

IT RAINED AND IT RAINED and it rained.

Year after year—within my decade-long relationship with it anyhow—Sole had been so parched that its surface curled back like a dried tongue and exposed red, bony gums of erosion. But now—when the international news crews were finally on hand to document its supposedly dry misery—the valley had apparently grown bored of being a desert and had decided to turn itself into a long, shallow lick of lake. Where once goats and donkeys hung rib-strung over bare ground, knee-high greenery appeared. Land that once danced, dry heaving with heat waves, now sung with the deadly whine of mosquitoes. While the surrounding land began to take on the hollow-eyed aspects of a glittering desert with stunted maize and bony cattle, Sole Valley grew small tidal waves and an infestation of frogs. Anything not big or strong enough to hold its head above the water took in a lungful of liquid and died, ballooned and stinking, in ditches and ravines. Many chickens and the odd small goat, surprised by so much unaccustomed water, died from disgust.

At Mum and Dad's fish and banana farm, eleven kilometers off the tarmac and downstream from the brothels, the biblically dead earth sprung green with a plague of luscious weeds. All day, day after day, battleship gray clouds gathered force over the Pepani Escarpment with such gravity that they threatened to oppress the sun. Insects tumbled out of the sky, with wings cracking and prickly legs. Christmas beetles shrilled. The wind picked up and tossed the leaves of the banana trees into shreds. The dogs hid their ears under their paws and looked anxious. The turkeys crouched under the wood stack and shat piles of reeking white, and the wild birds fell silent. The clouds menaced and massed.

Above my parents' camp, where the land sloped away into mopane pans, giant African bullfrogs that had lain in a tomb of concrete-solid earth for the last nine months exploded from the ground to mate and breed and roar for a few days before sinking back into the silence of the mud. They were enormous (as big as a soup bowl), Dracula-fanged and lurid yellow-green. They had black, lumpy ridges along their backs, like a pattern of ritualized scars from a nation of warriors.

Mum and I waded up to the top of the farm to inspect the frogs. Mum had read in her *Amphibians of Central and Southern*

Africa that they can live for up to twenty years. "Do you think they're any good for eating?" she asked.

"Mum!"

Mum rolled her eyes at me. "Don't be so squeamish, Bobo." She prodded one of the bullfrogs with her walking stick. "Come on," she said to it. "Hop. Let's have a look at those thighs."

"Mum!"

"My frog book was vague about their palatability."

"It probably didn't want to encourage people like you."

But then we found an old Tonga man collecting the frogs in a reed basket.

"See," said Mum, "you're overreacting, Bobo. I imagine lots of people eat them."

She asked the man if the frogs made good eating, but as she spoke no Tonga and the sekuru spoke no English, the conversation was reduced to pantomime. Mum hopping about and croaking while chomping on a fistful of fresh air and the ancient Tonga man blinking at Mum and shoving heaps of snuff at his nose, which he sneezed back at us in little toxic, black clouds. From inside the reed basket, the bullfrogs growled and hissed. Just as I was about to point out that this cultural exchange was getting all of us nowhere and some of us embarrassed, the sekuru grasped Mum's meaning. He unfurled his reed basket, seized a bullfrog by the throat, and lunged at us with it, grinning generously and gesturing that we should have it. The bullfrog barked and bared his fangs at me.

There is not, in any of the teach-yourself books of the local languages that line the shelves of my parents' bathroom bookshelf, the useful phrase "Thank you for your kind offer but I am a vegetarian."

Mum, who is an extreme omnivore, took the bullfrog back to the kitchen but lost her nerve at the last moment and set it free, whereupon it leaped under the firewood pile and glared at us with a mixture of alarm and disdain for the next several days. When it eventually died—which it did behind the pantry—it swelled up to the size of a soccer ball and Mum (who is of Scottish descent *and* has lived in Africa all her life and therefore cannot, both from habit and blood, waste anything at all) said, "What a pity it's so smelly now. It might have made an interesting lamp shade."

MUM AND DAD don't have a house to speak of on their fish farm, which is fine for most of the time. Usually, walls are an unnecessary barrier to what little breeze might condescend to lift off the Pepani River and swirl around our legs and shoulders as we sweat over our meals under the tamarind tree. The kitchen is a roof held up by four pillars and a half wall. The entire south side of the kitchen is taken up with a woodstove and a heap of firewood. The north side houses shelves of crockery and Mum's shortwave radio, perpetually tuned to the BBC World Service. The east is open to stairs that lead up through the garden to the workshop and offices, down which rain cascades in what might be a picturesque waterfall if it didn't back up into a small, greasy eyesore of a pond in the kitchen.

In this thoroughly quenching rainy season, Mum glared at the sky and said to it in a loud voice, intended for my father's deaf ears, "My roof leaks." And, "Can't you see, we don't have walls in our sitting room?" But Dad smoked his pipe in silence, absorbed in *Aquaculture Today*, apparently unaware that he was being rained upon until Mum said, "Tim, if you sit there much longer in that rain, you'll take root."

Then Dad folded up his magazine and said, mildly, "What's that, Tub? Time to get to work, is it?"

So, Mum and Dad covered their heads with tents of plastic and squelched up to the ponds to give mouth-to-mouth resuscitation to their fish, which, contrary to all logic, do not seem to like rain. And after lunch (a meal that consisted of several pots of tea and a banana) Mum and Dad trooped down to the end of the farm (shrinking hourly, as chunks of real estate were torn off by the powerful current and swept off down the Pepani to Mozambique) and stood dismal and worried on the riverbank, anxiously looking upstream, toward the brothels and taverns that make up the heart of the town of Sole. Clearly, if the rain kept up, we'd soon be knee-deep in waterlogged prostitutes and drunk truckers.

Day after day I kept to the shelter of the tamarind tree, in the company of the more sensible dogs, and drank cup after cup of tea. I read my way forward and backward through Mum's library and watched the sky for signs of the sun setting (however camouflaged by clouds) so that I might be excused the quick dash through the rain to the kitchen for a change of diet from tea to beer.

This kept up for five days. Finally, on the fifth evening, when the sun had wrapped up the day and folded it into the Pepani Escarpment for the night, we decided that the misery of our own company could not be endured for another moment. The rain had, for the time being, cleared off, so we drove out of camp to find a dry place to drink a cold beer.

MALIDADI LODGE IS THE sort of place that is more comfortable for its familiarity than for its amenities. Dogs curl up on the floor of the thatched open-air rondavel that houses the bar and a few metal picnic tables. The lights in the bar are unapologetically bright and thousands of insects dash themselves to death on the naked bulbs before sinking into the bar patrons' hair, glasses of beer, and clothes (a cleavage is a liability in this climate). The formal dining room is a lozenge-shaped room painted Strepsil green. It is a room dominated by a massive satellite television and half a dozen stark tables. Less lively by far than any of the other taverns we pass to get to the lodge,

Malidadi is a quiet, gently dissolving drinking hole mostly frequented by the tavern owners up the road (who are exhausted by their own noisy establishments) and by customs officials, businessmen, the local chief and his entourage, policemen, and commercial fishing guides.

On this night we—my parents and I—swelled the clientele of the bar by double (the other clients being the family of three that own the place).

I kissed everyone hello. Alex, the father, had just returned from the dead (by way of the Italian mission hospital) after a dose of particularly savage malaria. Marie, his wife, had given up smoking five or six years before, but she had smoked with such ferocity until then that she was still a pale shade of nicotine yellow and she was as fragile as a shard of ancient ivory. Katherine, the willow-thin daughter, pale and beautiful in a tragic, undernourished way, had been divorced for some years and she swallowed down her bitterness with repeated, tall glasses of neat vodka. They were generous people, made brittle with heat and disease.

"How are the children?" Marie asked.

"Fine," I replied, missing the two small creatures I had left back in Wyoming.

"You should bring them home to visit next time you come," Alex scolded.

"I will," I lied, slapping a mosquito off the back of my neck.

"And Charlie?" asked Katherine. "Is he well?"

"Very," I said.

"Do you like America?" Alex asked. I had lived in America seven years by then, but he still asked in the sort of doubting, tight voice you might use to ask someone "Do you like hell?" or "How is your incarceration?"

"I like it fine."

"We watch American shows on the satellite television," said Marie, as if that proved something.

We took our places around the bar. In acknowledgment of the proximity of Christmas, there was a strand of hairy green tinsel hanging above our heads. And above the cash register, a silver sign (scattershot with flyshit) read, MERRY XWAS (the *M* had twisted back on itself and no one had bothered to right it). A real tree frog (a large white one) crouched as still as marble on the rafter above a shelf of soldierly, brown brandy bottles— the frog wasn't a decoration, but he could have been.

Marie, who had been on the verge of taking herself off to bed-in-a-minute since I was last here a year ago, said, "I was just heading off," but instead she accepted another glass of sweet sherry (the kind that leaves a smeary trail on the edge of the glass) and added, "In a minute then." The dog at her feet, a handsome Rhodesian Ridgeback, had shredded legs from a crocodile attack earlier in the year. Marie kept a protective hand on his head, and he exuded a mild smell of flesh-rot. In the damp heat, the wounds from the crocodile attack were constantly wept open by the prying proboscises of flies. The dog did nothing to help matters with the insistence of his licking tongue.

We were on our second drink when the next round of rain came. It was dark outside by then so that we had not seen the clouds leave the edge of the escarpment and billow with stealth above our heads. There was a sudden cannon roll of thunder and then the world around us was a solid wall of water again. Conversation was impossible and there was only the task of drinking and of staring out at the silver-soaked night. But after half an hour of pounding rain, the storm subsided into a crack-ling hymn, like a stuck vinyl record left too long on the player. Our voices, once again, had power.

"That's some rain," said Dad, lighting his pipe and blowing a fragrant bloom of smoke at the rose beetles that were dive-bombing his brandy.

"Yup," said Alex. "I bet the gorge on K's place has flooded by now," and everyone squinted out in the shimmering night, which had taken on a dancing quality, as if we were able to confirm Alex's suspicion from the safety of a bar stool.

"Who's K?" I asked.

"Zimbabwean chap at the bend in the river," said Marie, pointing upstream toward the west. She took a swallow of sherry (her frailty is such that one expects to see the sherry light up her throat in a fire-red stream). "He's miles from anywhere," she said, "and in the rains—like this—his road is impossible. And when the rains really set in, he's stuck for real. Sometimes it's days and days when he can't get a lorry off his farm." She sucked in her lips and added, in a sad, knowing voice, "God, things must get pretty lonely on the farm for him."

Dad shook his head and grunted into his pipe, "Tough bugger, that."

"He doesn't drink," remarked Alex, which, in this part of the world, is newsworthy in and of itself.

"It's just as well," said Katherine. "He told me once that he's a violent drunk."

Marie said, "God forbid, he's a violent enough teetotaler."

"He's good-looking though," said Katherine, "but born again." Her head jerked up, the way an impala jerks its head to dislodge a persistent fly. "Isn't that typical? We finally get a half-decent-looking man down here and he turns out to be a bloody holy roller."

We went back to watching the rain play itself out against the dark night and drinking in silence.

Then Katherine said, "He almost killed some guy on the road to Lusaka the other day. A huge South African who wouldn't move his lorry because he was in a fight with some other driver who had nicked his side mirror. K had a lorry load of bananas that needed to get into town and this South African had stalled traffic for days on the escarpment. There were lorries all the way from there"—Katherine stretched her arms wide to indicate the hundred kilometers of tarmac road that stretch from the mountains to the valley—"to here." She flicked the ash off her cigarette decisively onto the floor and added, "K had the guy pinned up against his bull bars in about three seconds flat. He got his bananas to town, I can tell you that much."

"Did you see the fight?"

Katherine shook her head, and bent her neck to capture the end of her cigarette with her lips. She took a deep pull and blew smoke at me. "No," she said, "but everybody knows about it. The police think it's lekker having K here. Finally, someone who can sort out hassles. The police—you know how it is—never have transport, half of them are nearly dead from AIDS, they're scared to death of the truckers. They're not going to get themselves hurt trying to clear the escarpment. Now, if there's someone who needs to be sorted out, they just wait for K to arrive on the scene."

"He's a bloody good fighter," said Alex.

Dad grunted and knocked out his pipe on the heel of his shoe to show that he wasn't impressed.

But I said, "Really?"

"Well, that's what they say."

"Who's 'they'?"

Alex paused. "Come to think of it, K himself says."

Then Marie, fingering her gun, said, in a vague, unpromising way, "I'll be taking myself off to bed then in a minute," but she didn't move. Each member of this family carries a pistol to bed, and it is only when they are all armed (pistols wrapped in white canvas bank-bags) that they falter off into the night for their various chalets that are dotted around the grounds of the lodge. I keep waiting to hear about the string of accidents and misunderstandings that will lead, one day, to a major family shoot-out, like an episode of *Bonanza*-gone-*Addams-Family*.

Dad made a sound in the back of his throat and gave Marie an abbreviated bow. "Interesting evening. Thanks very much. Time for us to depart, Fullers all." He spoke with abrupt grace, as if he were some minor member of the royal family taking his leave from an obscure aboriginal ceremony in an overlooked corner of the British empire. Mum and I finished our drinks and hurried after him into the night. Out here, beyond the reach of the electric glare that spread from the rondaval, the witching darkness was so turbulent and vaporous with freshly hatched life and with its immediate contemporaries, death and decay, that the air seemed softly boiling with song, and with rustling wings and composting bodies.

Worms and War

Soldier at target practice

MIDMORNING THE FOLLOWING DAY, I was drinking orange juice at the picnic table and reading when the dogs suddenly spilled off my lap, as one indignant body, and scrambled up the steps toward the top of the camp in a hail of furious yelps. I looked up and there, under the arch (over which Mum had trailed a healthy vine of passion fruit), stood a man who seemed to straddle an unusually wide span of space for one person.

"Huzzit?"

"Hi," I said back, putting my book above my eyes as a shield against the high beat of light that scorched from the pale sun.

He said his name. I said mine. And then, for a long moment,

I stood by the picnic table looking up at him and he stood under the passion fruit vine looking down at me and neither of us said anything.

Even at first glance, K was more than ordinarily beautiful, but in a careless, superior way, like a dominant lion or an ancient fortress. He had a wide, spade-shaped face and wary, exotic eyes, large and khaki colored. His lips were full and sensual, suggesting a man of quick, intense emotion. His nose was unequivocal—hard and ridged, like something with which you'd want to plow a field. His thick hair was battleship gray, trimmed and freshly washed. He had large, even, white teeth.

He looked bulletproof and he looked as if he was here on *purpose*, which is a difficult trick to pull off in this woolly climate. He looked like he was his own self-sufficient, debt-free, little nation—a living, walking, African Vatican City. As if he owned the ground beneath his feet, and as if the sky balanced with ease on his shoulders.

He looked cathedral.

What is a man of your obvious beauty and talent doing in a place like this?

And then K took the steps that separated us, from the arch to the tamarind tree, in great strides like a man accustomed to consuming vast tracts of land in one helping. I noticed he was barefoot, but barefoot with a confidence born of familiarity rather than necessity, as if defying Africa to rear back and bite him. The dogs scattered and Mum's Barberton daisies bowed their heads as he marched toward me.

We faced each other over the picnic table. He stood, legs apart, as if trying to hold his balance against the unstable wobble of Earth's orbit. His smile, when it came, was surprisingly shy.

"Tea?" I asked.

K looked over his shoulder and hesitated.

"Mum and Dad are down at the tanks, sexing their fish."

"Doing what?"

"They're British," I reassured him. "I am sure it's less fun than it sounds."

K ran thick fingers through his hair. "Ja, well in that case . . . Cheers, I'd love some tea."

I went into the kitchen and shuffled the big black kettle over the hottest part of the fire, jiggling the branches over the glowing embers to give them fresh life. K leaned against one of the pillars that holds up the roof over the kitchen, like a piece of architecture himself; six foot two and 190 pounds. He watched me in silence. The branches spat and belched unruly smoke into the kitchen. My eyes spurted tears.

"Oh dear," I said, feeling ridiculous.

The turkey that had been roosting on the kitchen wall scuttled out into the garden gobbling her displeasure.

"Wood's wet," I explained.

K came over and crouched in front of the fire. He grasped a hot coil in his fingers and moved it, not quickly, but thoughtfully, as if arranging something artistically, to the front of the fire, then he pulled the branches to one side and blew gently over the wood. In a few moments a red-yellow flame lapped the bottom of the kettle.

"Wet wood's not a problem," said K. "Fire needs to *breathe*."

"Right."

"You can burn water grass if you just let the air in."

Perhaps I didn't look convinced because K said, "In Bangladesh, the curry munchers burn cowshit."

"Do they?" I said.

I brought the tray into the shade of the tamarind and K followed me from the kitchen. We sat opposite each other on camp chairs and the dogs picked their targets and scrambled up onto our laps.

"They said you'd be rained out by now," I said, pouring two cups of tea and handing one over to K.

"Who's 'they'?"

"At the lodge. We were there for a drink last night."

K smiled and rubbed his lips together. "Ja, ja," he said. "Well it's bloody sticky, but I could get through." He drank half the cup down and then sighed, as if the tea had fulfilled some thirst deeper than anything physical. Then he turned back to me and asked, "You don't live here anymore, do you? Where do you live now?"

"America."

K grunted, as if absorbing this information, then he said, "What do they call their munts over there?"

"You mean African Americans?"

"No, I mean your original munts."

"Native Americans," I said.

K laughed.

I frowned.

"But they still shot them in the back the first chance they got."

"Who?"

"The wazungu. It doesn't matter what they *call* them, they still shot them in the back and shoved them in compounds."

"Reservations."

"Same thing."

"It's complicated," I agreed.

"No, it's not."

I lit a cigarette.

"They hide behind their bullshit by calling it something else, but bullshit still smells like bullshit to me."

I scratched the crop of mosquito bites that was flourishing on my ankles.

"There's bad malaria here," K warned.

"I know."

"You should eat dried pawpaw seeds. Works better than anything for most hu-hoos. Even malaria."

"Really?" I said.

K blinked at me, then he suddenly leaned forward and, sweeping aside the formalities of small talk, seized my finger and led it to a place just under the sharp rise of his right cheekbone. "Feel that? Can you feel that?"

I couldn't feel anything, but I thought it impolite not to say yes.

K tightened his grip on the end of my finger. In the humidity, K's skin was slick with a light film of sweat. He had an organic, unadulterated smell, not at all unpleasant, but slightly acid-sweet, like salted tomatoes.

"Two years ago I started getting these moving, jumping lumps under my skin," K continued, pressing my finger deeper into his flesh. "There. See?"

I nodded.

"What do you think that is?"

I shook my head and reclaimed my finger. "Putsis?" I ventured, thinking of the eggs laid under the skin by flies in the rainy season that emerge later as erupting maggots.

K shook his head and pressed his lips together victoriously. "No."

"Worms?"

"Wrong again," said K.

"Pimple," I said. "I don't know. Boil, welt, carbuncle, locust."

K stared at me unsmiling, like a teacher waiting for an errant student to settle down before delivering the lesson of the day. He said, "It was a couple of years ago. I had just rescued this kitten—it was the rainy season and you know how these poor bloody kittens just wash up on the side of the road like drowned rats? Well, I found this kitten and brought it home and about a week later, these bumps start appearing everywhere. I thought I'd caught worms off the kitten, so I ate pawpaw seeds. No result. So I tried deworming pills Nothing. Except I got the trots. So then I soaked both of us in dog dip and I bloody nearly killed the poor kitten, but these lumps were still hassling me. They were here"—K pointed to his face—"and here" he clamped his hand behind his leg—"and here"—he held up his feet—"and here"—he lifted up his shirt and showed me his torso. "So then I bathed in twenty liters of paraffin and my ears bled for a month but still, these lumps kept twitching. I was going *benzi*, I tell you. Then I injected myself twice a day, every day for a week, with sheep dip, two cc's at a time. I thought maybe I had sheep maggots under my skin. But no. The sheep dip nearly killed me, I was in bed for a week, but the bloody things kept wiggling under my skin. So I burned my mattress, boiled my clothes, fumigated my bedroom, and cooked my shoes, but still, there they were. These hard, moving lumps under my skin. I finally went to the doctor and he gave me tablets that are supposed to kill worms that these people in West Africa get. I said to the doctor, 'This is Zambia, not bloody West Africa.' Six pills a day. They made me so sick, I thought I was going to die. There I was, back in bed, sick as a dog, with twitching lumps. Eventually, I went to a Chinese doctor in Lusaka, Mrs. Ho Ling—she diagnosed me with having inflamed nerve endings."

I could think of no better response than "Oh."

"It was just nerves," K told me, "too much stress. Too much war."

I assumed he meant The War—which around here would mean the second chimurenga, the Rhodesian War. I said, "But that's been over for twenty years."

K looked at me with surprise. "Oh no, I don't mean the hondo"—he used the Shona word for "war." "I mean the war with the wife. No, I don't think the hondo messed me up anything like the war with the wife did."

K poured himself more tea and started to talk in a tireless, arbitrary manner—about God, and war and divorce—as if a vast jumble of ideas surrounding his dissolving marriage and the nature of God and the state of the universe had been stored up for months in his mind, awaiting a patient audience. The thoughts were coming raw, unfiltered, and untested, directly from K's mind. He was like a lonely drunk who washes up to the bar after months without company and spills his soul to a complete stranger. Except that K was entirely sober.

While K talked, I studied his body. He was the kind of man whose body told as many stories as his mouth ever could. To begin with, there was the question of his hairlessness; his arms and legs looked as if they had been subjected to hours of waxing. Then, there were a number of scars to contemplate: a sliced head, some light cuts on his arm, a decorously scarred knee, and a round scar on the fleshy part of his calf that, if it was related to a similar scar above his ankle, was almost certainly the entry wound of a bullet. And finally, there were tattoos to consider, barely visible on his tawny-colored skin. On his left forearm he had a cupid (but it had been badly drawn and could also have been interpreted as a set of buttocks suspended between two billowing clouds). Above that, there was a portrait of a Viking. On his right forearm was a winged-sword symbol, like something that has been copied off a coat of arms. Above that, the words "A POS" had been written. The only men I know who have found it practical or necessary to have their blood group indelibly scratched into their limbs in blue ink have been soldiers in African wars.

So when K's torrent of unstrained observations and ideas had slowed to a halting trickle, I said, "Selous Scouts?" because even twenty years after the end of the second chimurenga, K had the build and attitude of a soldier from Rhodesia's most infamous, if not elite, unit.

K startled. For a moment I thought he was going to deny it but then he said, "Is it that obvious?"

"Oh no," I lied.

"No, not the Scouts," said K. "RLI. Rhodesian Light Infantry. Thirteen Troop."

The RLI had been Rhodesia's only all-white unit, highly trained white boys whose "kill ratio" and violent reputation were a source of pride for most white Rhodesians. Their neurotically graded system of racial classification apparently gave the Rhodesians a need to believe in white superiority in all things, even the ability to kill. During the worst years of the war, a quarter to a third of RLI members had been foreigners covertly recruited from Britain, West Germany, the United States, Canada, Australia, France, Belgium, New Zealand, and South Africa in a desperate attempt to ensure the unit remained lily-white.

K said, "I passed the selection course for the Scouts, but it wasn't my scene. I stuck with the troopies. 'The Incredibles.'"

"Oh?"

"I'm a hunter," K explained. "We did the hunting, we found the gooks. We had to sniff them out." K rubbed his knee as if an old injury had begun to twinge with the memory of combat. "Five years in Mozambique," he said. Then he added, "Of course by the end of the war, the RLI weren't hunters anymore. They were just killing machines—but by then I was out of it. I missed Operation Fireforce by about a year. You know, when ous were flown in and dropped on top of gooks for an almighty dustup—four, five times a day. Thankfully, I was out of it by then."

"How was the selection course?"

"For the Scouts, you mean?"

I nodded.

"You know what they called that training camp for the Scouts?"

I shook my head.

"Wasa Wasa. In Shona *wasa wafara* means, 'Those who die, die.'"

"So it was tough."

K shook his head. "Not so bad. They left four of us on an island in the middle of the lake for a couple of weeks. I've done worse. You weren't allowed anything except a shirt and a pair of shorts. When we got hungry enough we chased a baboon into the lake and drowned it."

"How'd that taste?"

K considered. "Well, if I had to do it all over again, I'd cook the fucking thing first."

"Ha."

Then K said, "Was it this?" He put his hand over the sword-symbol tattoo.

"Perhaps," I said.

K's voice sank. "This is the sign for the paraquedistas."

"For the what?"

"The Portuguese paratroopers," said K. "The Pork-and-Cheese jumpers, we used to call them. I tracked for them a few times."

"Portuguese from Portugal?"

K's chin gave an abrupt pop backward, which I took as a gesture of the affirmative.

"Were they good soldiers?" I asked.

"Yes, they were good. They could shoot straight. They had a pretty good kill ratio."

I took cover behind my teacup and said, "So did the RLI. Didn't they?"

K threw the dogs off his lap and dusted his hands. I thought he might get up and leave now.

Instead K said, "Ja, not bad." He leaned forward, fixed me in his lionlike gaze, and added in a soft voice, "Look, the life I've lived . . . shit, I wouldn't be here . . . *you* might not be here—a lot of people might not be here—if I, if we, couldn't slot people faster than they could slot us. I was good at what I did. . . . It was my job. I did it."

And then to my alarm I saw tears swell and tremble on the brims of K's eyelids. His nose grew pale-rimmed and tight.

"I'm sorry," I said.

K threw back his head. Two lines of tears were sliding freely down his cheeks.

I poured him some more tea and shoved the cup toward him. "Here, drink this."

K only stared into the branches of the tamarind tree. Tears had found their way into the dark folds on his neck, so that they shone in purple creases. Then K gave himself a little shake and wiped his face with the flattened palm of his hands, a gesture that I think of as being very African, the gesture of people who are not accustomed to the conveniences of napkins or towels. K sucked air in over his teeth and said, his voice watery, "It's a good thing the Almighty forgives all of us. It doesn't matter"—now he leaned forward and fresh tears sprung—"how much of a shit you are, how much you've destroyed. . . . The Almighty forgives us. He holds us all in His hands." K took a moment to compose himself before he could continue. "I just thank Him," he said finally.

And after that, a silence that might have been visible from space stretched in front of K and me. It was a splintering silence full of all the things I thought I already knew about K and all the things he thought I thought I knew about him.

"Anyway," he said. "That's all old news now, hey? The war's over. Best we forget about it. Dead and buried."

"Right," I said.

"I'm sorry you had to listen to me." He gave an embarrassed laugh. "I didn't mean to . . . No one comes out to my farm, so I don't see women very often. I mean white women. It catches me off guard."

"Don't apologize."

K stood up and tugged the end of his shorts, "Ja. Well, I should probably head back to the farm and see what those Einsteins have been up to in my absence."

By now, it was early afternoon. It was the slow part of day

when heat gathers like fingering thieves into your body and steals energy and desire and initiative.

I stood up. "I imagine Dad's still down at the fish tanks if you wanted to see him."

"No." K stretched. "I didn't come to see your dad in particular. Just a white face in general. Any white face will do." He smiled. "Mission accomplished."

I trailed up the steps to the arch after K. The dogs, who were belly-up on the chairs or splayed out on the lawn, watched us leave the camp—they did not move. Anything with a brain and with any feeling at all was staying as still as it could. Only the flies spun and buzzed and twirled and dive-bombed.

"You must come out and see me on my farm sometime," said K as he climbed into his pickup. "How long are you out here for?"

"I go back to the States the week after Christmas," I said.

"Well, then there's plenty of time. Come and see my bananas."

I nodded. "Maybe," I said, but my voice was drowned out by the revving engine.

K gave a dismissive wave and turned his attention to the road.

I watched the pickup back out of the yard and, in a paste of mud, grind up the slick driveway. Mud splattered the side of the vehicle and flew out behind the back wheels in little red pellets. A cascade of egrets, rattled by the commotion, erupted up out of the green grass and banked around to the fish ponds above the camp, their wings paper-white against gray clouds.

Words and War

Mum and Dad's shower and bath

WHEN I WAS A LITTLE GIRL, spinning around in the cycle of violence that I understood, only very vaguely, as Rhodesia's war of independence, I used to have a recurring dream that I was being abducted by a massive crow; it scooped me up from the garden where I had been playing and flew with me to Mozambique, where it dropped me on a land mine. And then I would wake up screaming, still floating toward the mine (absurdly slowly, because it was the mid-1970s and I was, at the time, fond of a pair of large hand-me-down bell-bottom jeans, which served the dual purpose, in my dream at least, of fashion statement and parachute).

The night after I first met K, I had that same old war dream and I woke up, choking on a scream, bell-bottoms billowing by my ears and the tinny taste of helplessness (the taste that comes before a scream) in my mouth. I lay in the darkness feeling my heart smack against the edge of my ribs until, at last, thinking I would not be able to get back to sleep, I let myself out of my mosquito net and into the insect-creaking night beyond its lacy comfort. I felt my way down the uneven steps (toes curled against frogs and centipedes) and toward the picnic table, which lurked shadowy and indistinct under the deep-forever night that leaked through the branches of the tamarind tree.

The rain, as Dad had predicted, had stopped by now and left the air a little cooler. Where the clouds had ragged apart, the sky reached back until the beginning of time, black poured on black. I groped around the picnic table for Dad's cigarettes and scraped a chair back. One of Mum's guinea fowls purred at me from its perch as I sat down.

"Just don't take me to Mozambique," I told the guinea fowl, blowing a funnel of blue smoke at it.

The guinea fowl spluttered and the wind gave a breathy sigh. Raindrops shook off the leaves of the tamarind tree and plopped onto my shoulders and bare legs. I shivered and pulled one of the little dogs onto my lap.

Dad woke up just before dawn and came down to the picnic table. He wore a length of bright chitenge cloth around his waist, above which his body gleamed white in the shape of his shirt, his arms and neck burned a ruddy brown. He said, "Sleep all right?"

"Fine."

"Leave any for me?" he asked, shaking the box of cigarettes.

"One or two."

Dad coughed and lit a cigarette. "How long have you been down here?"

"Hours," I said.

"Then why didn't you make the bloody tea yet?"

"I had a nightmare."

Dad pinched the end of the match out between his thumb and forefinger. "Nightmare make you afraid of the kettle?"

"Nope."

"Miss your electric stove in America?" asked Dad, breathing smoke at me.

"Maybe."

Dad made a fire and boiled water, grunting in a soft, mildly complaining way as he laid a tray with cups, a jug of milk, sugar, the cigarette caught in the corner of his mouth. Then we moved up to the top of the camp, sat on the edge of Mum's flower bed, and watched the graying dawn stroke mist through the rain-startled bush, and a snaky wisp of cloud rise off the Pepani River. We were quiet for a long time, drinking and smoking.

Then I asked, "Do you ever have nightmares about the war?"

"Nope."

I lit the last cigarette. "Liar."

Dad cleared his throat.

I said, "I hear you shouting in your sleep sometimes."

"I'm not asleep. I'm shouting at the bloody dogs."

"You're shouting, 'Heads down!' and 'Shit, we're hit!'"

Dad poured himself more tea and shook the empty cigarette box. "It wasn't much of a war," he said at last.

"Were you ever scared?"

"Scared to death. Bored to death. Both."

I had seen my father go off to fight in the war. He didn't have to go very far from our farm near Umtali, on Rhodesia's border with Mozambique. He walked to the end of the driveway, where he was picked up in a camouflage-painted Land Rover and taken off with five other farmers to the hills above our house, where they crept about for a couple of weeks hoping not to get noticed by the enemy. My father was called up into the Police

Anti-Terrorist Unit (PATU), an outfit known colloquially as Dad's Army.

"Cannon fodder was what we were," Dad said. "We were just a bunch of bumbling farmers buggering around in the bush without much of a clue. We were lucky to get out of the war without shooting each other, let alone the bloody gooks."

Dad gave up guns—even for hunting or crop protection—after the war. So now he and his men chase hippos and elephants off the bananas with gongs and branches of fire and Dad's brave, thin shouts ragged in the thick, Pepani night, "Come on, you buggers! Off my bananas!"

I said, "K was in the RLI."

"Really?"

"That's what I thought at first too." I took a sip of tea.

"Ha." Dad shook his head. "In any case, those baskets were tough, I wouldn't want to argue with one of those troopies."

The soldiers in the RLI were called troopers (or, colloquially, troopies). The guerrillas nicknamed them MaBruka because the troopers wore very short shorts. Brookies, in Rhodesian slang, are little girls' underwear.

"Did you believe in the war?"

"What?"

"Did you think it was right?"

Dad said, "Fergodsake, Bobo. The sun's not even over the top of the bananas."

"Well?"

"No."

"Then why did you fight?"

"Call-up."

"You could have been a conscientious objector."

"A what?"

"A pacifist."

"No, I couldn't."

"Why not?"

"I was there and the war was there and that's what I had to do. That's what we all had to do—they didn't give you a choice. It was stay and fight or get out. We would have lost the farm. We would have lost everything."

"We lost the farm anyway," I pointed out.

Dad grunted. "In any case, I wasn't going to sit the war out and let some other poor bastard get snuffed on my account."

"Do you regret it?"

Dad stood up and rubbed his belly. "I'm going to have a shower and then I am going to see my fish," he said.

"Why won't you talk about it?"

"Nothing to talk about."

TALK KILLS, the posters above bars from the Eastern Highlands to Wankie had declared during the war. LOOSE TONGUES COST LIVES. I can just about guarantee Dad never killed anyone with his tongue.

I said, "It might do you good to talk about it."

Dad grunted. "I tell you what would do me good."

"What?"

"If my daughter left her old man a few bloody cigarettes for his breakfast." He tromped off to the shower—a loose grass enclosure at the top of the camp that was open to the sky and occasionally sagged open at the edges, revealing glimpses of the soapy, white body within. A silver bucket was suspended by a rope pulley over a circle of red gravel, a rickety bush-pole table held a candle (in a green wine bottle), a dish of soap, and a bottle of shampoo. Frogs and snakes nested in the grass fence and scorpions peered with glinting black eyes from the drain. The dogs trotted after Dad, looking forward to their morning encounter with the shower's variety of wildlife. In a few moments I heard the squeak of the bucket as it was lowered over my father, then a gush and Dad muttering under his breath at the shock of cold water. One of the Jack Russells came trotting out with her tail raised in victory and a lizard clenched between her jaws.

. . .

BY THE MID-1960S, all but a handful of African countries had gained independence from their European settlers. The Southern Rhodesian government, led by Ian Smith, in a panic lest the British prime minister turn their country over to the Africans too, made a Unilateral Declaration of Independence (UDI) on November 11, 1965. Under UDI whites retained power and black Rhodesians remained unable to vote. Wrex Tarr, Rhodesia's resident wag, reflected the casualness with which whites regarded this momentous decision by tagging UDI a "Universal Declaration of Indifference." A state of emergency was declared—but this was more a way to keep uppity blacks in line than to placate satiated whites.

Britain and the United Nations Security Council responded to Smith's move by slamming economic sanctions on the rogue state, and black Rhodesian nationalists began preparing for war, training in countries that were sympathetic to their cause: Zambia, Ghana, Tanzania, China, North Korea, and the Soviet Union. For a time, the nationalist guerrillas dispatched into Rhodesia were quickly captured and killed by government forces; they were, as one white farmer put it, "only a pinprick in our sides" and "merely garden boys." But, in 1972, the rebels intensified their war. No longer operating from beyond Rhodesia's borders, they infiltrated the northeast of the country, caching arms near Centenary and Mount Darwin, and living in and off the local villages. From these bases, they attacked white farmers and intimidated their laborers; they laid mines and set ambushes. The "garden boys," it turned out, weren't nearly as inept or inefficient as the whites had painted them, and they were serious about gaining their independence.

What made the Rhodesian War almost unique among wars for independence in Africa was that both sides—white and black—considered themselves indigenous to the land. By the start of the war in the in the late sixties, the total population of the country hovered at around 5 million—of that, 230,000 people (at most) were white (or, in appearance, obviously "white") and were considered by the government to be politically and socially more important than any other race in the country. There was also a small population of Indians and coloureds—coloureds were defined by Rhodesians as people with mixed blood—who ranked in the power base slightly above the blacks, but still far below the whites. By the end of the war, all able-bodied white and coloured men between the ages of seventeen and sixty were on permanent or semipermanent call-up "in defense of Rhodesia."

The guerrillas belonged in one of two forces—ZANLA (Zimbabwe African National Liberation Army) or ZIPRA (Zimbabwe People's Revolutionary Army). The Mashona joined the ZANLA forces and made for Mozambique. The Matabele joined the ZIPRA forces and hid in Zambia. Whenever the two forces met, the rivalry that existed between the Matebele and the Mashona, and that preceded their common hatred of the whites, erupted in skirmishes.

The regular Rhodesian army had two battalions—the all-white RLI and the all-black (but white-officered) Rhodesian African Rifles (RAR). The Rhodesians took advantage of the existing enmity between the indigenous nations by dividing the RAR into Mashona and Matabele regiments. When there was trouble in the Matabele areas of Rhodesia, the Mashona troops were sent. When there was trouble in the Mashona area, the Matabele troops were sent.

It is tempting—because it is less complicated—to think of the Rhodesian War as being about right and wrong, black and white. The truth is, of course, blurrier than that. On the whole, it was a war of race, but it was also a war of clashing nations and conflicting ideals. The whites claimed they were defending a way of life, that they were defending the country against communism, that they were protecting "our munts from themselves." In the late seventies, when the Rhodesian War was at its most desperate and brutal, some of the rest of Africa was in the throes of a postcolonial massacre. The liberators of many African states had learned too well the vile lessons of their erstwhile oppressors and had turned their jaws—sometimes literally—onto their own people.

Blaine Harden, the *Washington Post* bureau chief in sub-Saharan Africa from 1985 to 1989, offers up a smattering of examples of the bizarre behavior of some of Africa's leaders in the late seventies in his *Africa: Dispatches from a Fragile Continent:*

> Uganda's Amin declared himself King of Scotland, sent a cable to Richard Nixon wishing him a "speedy recovery from Watergate," and ordered white Britishers to carry him on a throne-like chair into a reception for African diplomats. Before he was toppled in 1979, his troops killed an estimated quarter-million people and ripped Uganda, once the most prosperous country in East Africa, to pieces. Bokassa installed himself in 1977 as "emperor" of the Central African Republic in a diamond-studded, Napoleonic-style ceremony that cost $22 million, one quarter of his country's national revenue. After his overthrow two years later, he was convicted, among other things, of murdering members of his army, poisoning his grandchild, and taking part in the killing of at least fifty children who had refused to wear school uniforms to school. At Bokassa's trial in 1987, the prosecutor said there was not enough evidence to convict the former emperor of cannibalism. One of Bokassa's former cooks, however, testified that his boss kept corpses in a walk-in refrigerator and that Bokassa had once asked him to serve one for supper.

Rumors of cannibalism and chaos in independent Africa were, of course, rich fodder for Rhodesia's propaganda machine. White Rhodesians, the government argued, had only to look north to see what was in store for them if they allowed the blacks to run the country. Pointing to examples of brutal and inept dictators north of the Zambezi, Ian Smith felt justified in calling black Rhodesians the "happiest blacks in Africa."

The black guerrillas were fighting for their freedom—the freedom to vote, to own land, to receive a good and equitable education, and to walk the streets of their own country without fear. The liberation forces were regaled by their leaders with a picture of Rhodesia as it had been in precolonial times: an era of prosperity and pride, of great architecture and stunning art. It had been a time of self-sufficiency, freedom, and fairness. It had been, above all, a time when the great Mashona farmers had been allowed to cultivate their own land and when the brave Matabele warriors and cattlemen had been allowed to defend their own livestock against lions and theft.

Both sides claimed to be morally right.

Acts of stunning bravery and of spectacular cowardice were committed on both sides. Neither side was exempt from atrocities. Both sides were brutalized by the experience. The guerrillas terrorized villagers, raped civilian women, killed alleged "sell-outs," murdered innocent families, and desecrated churches; the Rhodesian Security Forces tortured and murdered their prisoners, burned villages, raped civilian women "sympathizers." And at the end of it all, soldiers of all colors and political persuasions were left washed up and anchorless in some profound way—like the guilty survivors of a natural disaster. War is not the fault of soldiers, but it becomes their life's burden.

Anyone who has existed on the soil on which a war is fought knows the look of the returned soldier—the haunted look of someone who has seen more than his fair share of horror. People who have inflicted pain, who have destroyed, who have been in pain and been destroyed. People whose words for killing reflect the casualness with which they have learned to view the act:

"scribbled," "culled," "plugged," "slotted," "taken out," "drilled," "wasted," "stonked," "hammered," "wiped out," "snuffed."

By the late seventies, the Rhodesian government was finding it more and more difficult to finance its efforts and to persuade the increasingly weary population that this gruesome war was a viable alternative to black majority rule. In December 1979, the United States and Britain brokered a cease-fire, which led to all-party elections in 1980.

It is a measure of how brainwashed white Rhodesians were that they were stunned to hear, on March 4, 1980, that Robert Mugabe, a leader of one of the guerrilla factions and a Marxist terrorist—a man whom many of them had never even heard of—had won an absolute majority in the parliamentary elections. As blacks celebrated in the streets of newly independent Zimbabwe, the white residents who had just fought, and lost, a long and bitter war stood by in appalled silence.

In their book, *Rhodesians Never Die,* Peter Godwin and Ian Hancock wrote that the Rhodesian authorities estimated that there were 20,350 war-related deaths in Rhodesia between December 1972 and December 1979. Fewer than 500 white civilians were killed while at least 7,000 black civilians and 10,000 guerrillas were killed. Over 1,000 members of the Security Forces were killed (under half of them white). Black civilian deaths were certainly underestimated and high casualties inflicted on black Rhodesian refugees in external raids (in Mozambique and Zambia) were ignored altogether. The African population bore the brunt of the war, but the European minority shed proportionately more blood. All came out of the war scathed in some way.

What is harder to document are the nonfatal casualties of the war. The victims of suicide (sewerage pipe, it was jokingly called), the alcoholics, the drug addicts, the homeless, the psychologically damaged, the people who (knowing nothing else *but* war) became mercenaries in other African wars (and ended their lives in South Africa, Mozambique, Angola, Somalia, or Namibia). The horror of the war remained largely unspoken and unacknowledged in the celebration of the freedom fighters' victory. The whites either left the country, and sometimes the continent, or melted back into everyday life and tried to adjust to majority rule. The blacks found that independence had brought them little of the freedom and power they had been promised.

My family left Zimbabwe in 1982, when I was thirteen, a little over two years after the end of the war. We headed first for Malawi and then, when Dad's contract on a tobacco plantation was up in that country, to Zambia. As part of the physical act of forgetting those years and the Rhodesian land for which my mother and father had fought so inadequately, and so pointlessly, we burned everything that might implicate us in that struggle.

A bonfire at the top of that farm near Umtali turned into ashes the T-shirts that declared "Rhodesia Is Super, Especially Umtali," "Come to Umtali and Get Bombed," and "Burma Valley Operation Thrasher." We burned our Wrex Tarr *Zonke Chilapalapa* record (featuring "A Terrorist's Lament" and "Picannini Red Riding Hood") and our Clem Thollet "We Are All Rhodesians" tape, and we watched our propaganda magazines (distributed by the Rhodesian Ministry of Information) spiral into smoke. Then we packed up the dogs and cats and as many possessions as would fit in the back of a Land Rover and we headed north into African countries that had been independent for nearly twenty years.

WHEN DAD CAME OUT of the shower, he said, "Water's nice and cold. Why don't you hop in?"

"I'm thinking."

"Do you want a piece of advice from your old father?"

"Not really."

"Don't look back so much or you'll get wiped out on the tree in front of you."

Curiosity and Cats

Dad

BY THAT AFTERNOON, the rain had returned. And by late
evening, when we sloshed down to the end of the farm to see
what remained of its west bank, the river had abandoned all
pretense of making its way toward Mozambique in a stately
manner and had gathered up its skirts and was racing with unseemly haste, tumbling great chunks of Fuller real estate with it
in the process. The island in front of the watchman's hut was

washed away from its foundations and could be seen sailing hurriedly down the Pepani.

Two enterprising young crocodiles, flushed out of the roiling river, worked their way through the bananas to the breeding pond at the top of the farm and inhaled hundreds of fish before they were discovered by Mum.

"Now that," she said as the pond was drained, "I really cannot allow."

The crocodiles sank guiltily into the shrinking muddy puddle. But Mum hardened her jaw. "Nope," she said, "no clemency."

Erasmus, the man whose job it was to take care of the breeders, and who had been a poacher before he found employment with Mum and Dad, told Mum, "I have a good trick for killing crocodiles. It is only that I need a torch and a gun."

"For heaven's sake," said Mum, sniffing. "Just bonk the little blighters on the head and bring me their hides."

Then we hurried back through the rain to the camp, sat huddled under the shelter of the tamarind tree, and tried to ignore the yelps and shouts that wafted down through the persistent rain from the top of the farm.

Eventually Erasmus, looking like the sole survivor of a catastrophic mud slide, appeared with two crocodile skins and laid them on the veranda wall for Mum's approval. Mum inspected them and said, "Pity about all the holes. They might have made quite a sweet pair of shoes."

Dad lit his pipe and said, "Still got all your fingers, Erasmus?"

"Bwana?"

Lightning blanketed the sky and turned everything an eerie shade of pale blue for a moment. Thunder swelled around us, as if the belly of the earth were growling.

Mum said, "Thank you, Erasmus. You'd better knock off now."

Dad said, "You'd better salt those skins like mad, or they'll start stinking the place up."

Mum said, "I might pin them up around the ponds as a warning to other crocodiles."

Dad said, "I'm going to Lusaka tomorrow. Anyone need anything?"

"Should we treat ourselves to a nice fat turkey for Christmas this year?"

"What's wrong with those things that keep crashing around the garden? Why don't we eat one of them?"

"Those are Atatürk and Isabelle, and they're not for eating," said Mum. "Too tough by now anyway."

It was quite true that Mum's pet turkeys had been more than usually exercised by the frequent appearance of snakes and monitor lizards and by the constant unwanted attention of the dogs.

"Crocodile tail?" Dad tried.

"Not very Christmassy," said Mum. "Go and see the Greek fellow at Cairo Butchery. You might be able to swap some fish for a bird."

Dad sighed. "All right. What about you, Bobo?"

"I don't think I can stomach Lusaka," I said, thinking of the crush of traffic and the blistering Christmas decorations flapping from the shop windows, everything turgid and overblown. I find the forced cheer of the holiday season depressing in northern climes, but the tropical equivalent is almost unbearable. And I thought of myself half suffocated and sweating, permanently assigned to guard the car while Dad negotiated with the Greek butcher. "I'll stay in the valley," I said.

Mum said, "You could always help me sex the fish."

I flinched, "No thanks, Mum," and said to Dad, "Maybe you could drop me off at K's farm. I'll go and look at his bananas."

Dad threw me a sharp look from above his pipe.

"What?" I said.

"Nothing."

"I'm curious," I said.

"You know what they say?"

"What?"

Dad tapped his pipe and cleared his throat. "Curiosity scribbled the cat."

"Well," I said, "aren't you curious?"

"Nope."

THE NEXT MORNING, shortly after six, Dad stopped the pickup at a signpost advertising a school, a church, and K's farm. "This is it," he said. "Just follow the signs."

"How far?"

Dad shrugged. "I don't know. I've never been there." He handed me a packet of cigarettes and a box of matches. "Here."

"Thanks."

"It's on the Chabija River somewhere. Ten or fifteen kilometers, I think."

"Okay." I looked out into the vast stretch of Africa that swept in front of me, a rolling belly of land as far as I could see, interrupted by the odd stark hill and bands of dense trees. The occasional throb of smoke chugged up out of the expanse, indicating the presence of a lonely village. There was no sign of a commercial farm, usually distinguishable by a better-than-usual road, tobacco barns, rows of gum trees (grown to fuel flue-cured Virginia tobacco or for fence posts).

"Everyone here knows him. Just ask for Mr. Banana."

"All right."

Dad eased the pickup back onto the tarmac. His brown arm wedged out of the window of the cab as he spun away into the distance. The car looked too small and feeble against the space that billowed above it and the great expanse of mopane forest that spread out on either side of it. Very quickly, the pickup became a shimmying white dot against the black road, and then it was gone. I started to walk.

The road to K's farm was really more of a fitful dirt track

than a road in the conventional sense of the word, an irregular cut into the bush, soupy with the recent rain. Within minutes, gluey clay stuck on the soles of my shoes, until I was teetering on a platform of the stuff. I took my shoes off and walked barefoot, letting sausages of mud ease between my toes. As soon as the sun tipped the edge of the horizon and fingered through the mopane trees, the air grew languid with the kind of clammy heat that promises worse to come. On either side of me, there were wallowing settlements—clusters of huts and thorn-branch kraals—exhaling in the post-rain morning sun. There was a salty, sinewy smell of smoked goat meat on the air, mixed with the scent of damp thatch and the raw, churning smell of sun on wet manure. Small, nose-and-eye-seeking mopane flies clustered on my face and congregated in the sweat-cut creases in my neck and behind my knees. Children, desperately malnourished and filthy, made a wake of shouting chorus behind me, practicing their English with triumphant insistence: "How are you? What is your name? Where are you going? Give me your shoes!"

I passed the church—a stern white building set apart from the sporadic jumble of fields and the disarray of huts that made up the villages along here. Its blue wooden doors were locked and its windows, bare narrow slots, were too high for me to see into. The school, a ramshackle affair, was set back from the church on an eroding hill. Next to it, a muddy soccer field lay waterlogged and churned. Two goats and a donkey were nibbling grass near one of the goalposts.

I kept walking and eventually crossed a wide, sandy river and then a reed-spiked wetland, and now the track narrowed to a threaded ribbon through the trees, barely wide enough to allow the passage of a lorry. The villages had thinned to small settlements hacked out of the bush surrounded by balding patches of flooded millet and maize. Chicken coops, suspended from stilts, tilted in the clay, threatening to topple over altogether. At one of these outposts, an old man shuffled out of the bush, tightening a string around the top of ragged trousers. We greeted each other. The old man rubbed rheumy eyes and spat prolifically—he looked and sounded as if he had been smoked over a wood fire for a long, long time.

"Mr. Banana?" I asked, pointing into the ever thickening country ahead of me.

The old man adjusted his trousers and cleared his throat. *"Ee,"* he agreed, and then indicated that he'd like a cigarette. We stood together in the morning sun for the space of one smoke; then he turned and scuffed off into his hut and I returned to the track.

I walked for another kilometer or two and then the feeble track that I had been following abruptly forked, the broader part of it peeling off to the left and the right petering out to an almost indiscernible footpath. The trees were varied and enormous here, great black-barked msasas and wide-bellied winter thorns. I took the left fork and kept walking.

It was late morning by the time my ear caught the sound of men shouting in unison. It was the sound that I associate, in Zambia at least, with men doing work that in much of the rest of the world is done by machines. I hurried toward the noise and there, a few kilometers before the boundary to his farm, were K and a span of laborers. The men were stripped to the waist and were trying to shore up the greasy banks of a steep gorge with the great arms of a mopane tree. K was shouting orders in Shona and the men were scrambling and slithering in response, crying words of exertion and exhortation to one another: "Pamsoro, pamsoro, pamsoro! Sumudza!"

The gorge was the kind of deep-throated slit into the earth that hosts seasonal, lorry-swallowing flash floods. K informed me in a series of breathless shouts that it had spilled its banks in the night and had torn loose the bridge that once spanned it. Now, just twelve hours after the end of the rainstorm, the water had subsided to a series of sedate pools—even though whole limbs of trees hung where they shouldn't, debris had been thrown high up onto land, and what was left of the bridge was being worn, as a necklace, by a fever tree.

I scrambled down the bank and waded through a coffee-colored pool. K came to the bank and gave me a hand up the other side. I was aware that I was disheveled to the point of dissolving: sweaty, mud-spattered, and flustered. K did not seem at all affected by the heat. Indeed, with his great expanse of hairless skin, he seemed especially modified to suit the climate. He helped the men press three more branches of a tree into the bank and then he stood back. One man came up to K and they spoke together in Shona, their voices low and urgent. Then the man nodded and slid into the water below the level of the bridge.

K turned to me. "So you came to see the farm?"

I nodded. "I hope it's okay. You look busy."

"Do you want some tea?"

"I don't want to interrupt you."

"No, it's okay. Michael's here. He's my farm manager."

Michael—the man with whom K had just been speaking—crawled up from the riverbed. He was a tall muscular man whose age it was hard to discern, since his face was remarkably clear and unlined while his hair was quite gray. His smile was easy and vivid and belied worried, tired eyes. We shook hands and I told him who I was. Michael nodded—he had heard of my father. And then we swapped the inevitable stories of who we knew in common, which turned out to be more people than I had expected. Half of the men and women on the fish farm were apparently related to Michael, while one of the market women I had befriended in Sole was his aunt.

Then we took our leave and K led me to his pickup. He said that he had never seen such rain since moving here.

"When was that?" I asked.

K opened the passenger door for me. "Five years ago." He went around to the driver's side and let himself into the cab; then he slipped the car into gear and we surfed off the muddy bank onto what passed for a road. The engine roared and whined and the tires seethed, the car veered to the side and spun, mud flicked up. K changed gears and the car suddenly surged forward and I found myself flung back. I hung on to the door handle and stared out of the windscreen as the world slashed past me in a violent explosion of color. I had the impression of towering woodland opening up onto a surprising stretch of shaggy savannah and then a jumble of riverside foliage.

Suddenly, the bush peeled away from us and an electric fence glinted sharply in the sun. K turned and shouted at me, "The farm starts here."

I nodded. We had broken through the chaos of the rain-battered forest onto something almost eerily neat, combed flat, and pinned down. Here, the road was properly graded and graveled, so that the pickup stopped revving and swerving and began to hum along with ease over the wet but firm surface. Lines of soldierly bananas in four distinct blocks made way for a precisely tended vegetable garden and a shade-cloth house of domestic garden plants. Small palm trees jutted their heads up behind carefully landscaped arrangements of shrubs and flowering plants, and a long, clipped lawn swept up from a fence to the workshop and road.

Beyond the farm, the untidy virgin bush that we had just come through waved back at us rude and exuberant. "This was all shateen," said K, sweeping his hand across the obedient plantations of bananas, "all completely wild. I had to clear it one acre at a time. You should have seen the snakes in here"—K circled his thumb and forefinger around his wrist—"as thick as this."

We stopped at a stand of bananas. "Come and see," he said. I followed K into the cool, gloomy world below the wide canopy of banana leaves. The light filtered green and dense from above. The ground below us was bare of any vegetation except for the thick, pulpy trunks of the banana trees.

K kicked the ground with his toe. "See this?" he asked, turning up some grayish soil. "I send the gondies up into the hills to raid the caves for batshit. It's the best fertilizer on earth."

The air was bitten with a nitrous reek, like chicken manure, that was mixed with the scent of rotting banana leaves and wet, worm-turned earth. These smells were all the more powerful for being trapped under the almost solid lid of leaves above our heads.

K kept walking, and as we ventured deeper into the bananas, sounds from beyond were increasingly muffled, until at last there was silence, except for the sound of K's bare feet padding along the weed-free, flattened ground and me stumbling unevenly behind him.

Then K stopped and held up his hand. "Hear that?"

"What?"

"Nothing."

I held my breath. "Nothing," I agreed.

"Where else can you go in this country without hearing anything at all? No insects, no birds, no gondies. Nothing."

The air felt suspended and bitter; air that is not used to being chilled and so sinks in on itself and becomes deadened.

"It's my church," said K. "Sometimes, I come and kneel in here." K lifted his hands and I half expected him to fall to his knees in rapture. "Utter peace," he breathed. "Hear that? Complete serenity."

"Yes."

K turned and smiled. "I just wanted you to feel that," he said. "Now, I must make you some tea."

Dogs and Curiosity

Road to K's farm

K'S HOUSE TURNED out to be a single cement bedroom—low and bleak, like a prison cell—with a veranda attached to it overlooking a view of an island at a bend in the Chabija River. Here, the river turned back on itself as if to admire its own languid journey toward the Pepani, which it joined a few kilometers downstream. At the bend, the riverbank towered thirty or forty feet high—a sheer wall of red clay exploding with carmine bee-eaters whose nest holes bored into the cliff and whose calls echoed across the water, "terk terk." The river was the color of milky tea, unsettled with the recent rain. Three hippos had set up house off the point of an island in front of K's bedroom and they occasionally erupted with complaining shouts of "Hot! It is too damn hot today," then blew a fountain of spray from their nostrils or wagged manure into the water.

A tiny bathroom, militarily stark in its simplicity with a small washbasin and a loo, was attached to the bedroom. A bed, a chair, a table, and a metal closet made up the bedroom's furniture. On the wall, K had hung some wildlife prints and framed photographs of various stiffly posing people of several generations, whom I took to be members of his family. Next to K's bed, on the little wooden table, were a leather-bound Bible and a small plastic clock. A tiny fan had been bolted onto the window ledge (there was no windowpane, just a metal grille and mosquito gauze with a reed mat that could be rolled down in heavy rain). There was no way to communicate with the world beyond Chabija from here; no phone, no computer, no radio, no television.

The kitchen was a separate, bare-boned building, which could be reached via a brick path from the bedroom. It was a simple affair, three half walls along the front and sides and a whole wall along the back holding up an asbestos-sheet roof. A shelf along the back wall held a kettle, a pot, a pan, a few plates and cups. A gas stove and a sink took up most of the front wall. A washing line hung over the woodstove, bright with K's shirts and shorts. Three dogs and a cat were splayed out on the floor. The dogs were named Sheba, Mischief, and Dispatch.

"Dispatch?"

K said, "The gondies call him Dizzy-patch." K tickled the dozing dog with his toe and the dog flipped onto his feet with a soft growl and then, seeing K, began to wag his tail and grin. "He's a good dog," said K, patting the dog's head, "incredible watchdog."

I said, "Hello Dizzy-patch."

Dispatch backed into K's legs, flattened his ears, and bared his teeth at me. He was a low, squat dog, the kind that steals up to you from behind—a ground-scraping shadow—and sinks his teeth into your leg before you've seen or heard him coming.

K prepared the tea himself. "I don't like to have gondies around the house," he said. "I have someone in the morning to clean and do laundry and the gardener comes in the morning to water and weed and then"—K indicated the gate with his head— "if anyone wants me they must hit the gong by the gate."

I slid along the kitchen wall, keeping a wary eye on Dispatch, and followed K down to a picnic table overlooking the river, where we sat with cups balanced on our laps. The cat crouched over a saucer of milk and the dogs lined up for their biscuits (sugary Zimbabwean tea biscuits sold at the Sole market by Michael's aunt). K had fried battered okra, which we ate with salt, licking our fingers against the grease.

On the other side of the Chabija, I could see a village perched on the riverbank. It was a series of huts facing toward K's camp, their doors like yawning mouths into the gloomy interiors that lay anonymously within. Sitting around the outside of the huts, the curved shape of men, seated on low stools, focused on playing a game. Beyond that, two men in ragged shorts were laboriously mending a fishing net spread out on the ground between them. A woman was kneeling in a clearing near a small cooking hut, pounding maize, her body falling and rising from the hips, her arms outstretched and gripping the pestle. Children and goats and chickens fell in and out of shadows.

"That village has sprung up since I've been here," said K. "Before I came, there was nothing here at all. No road, no village. Nothing. Now I have about twelve families living over there and about two thirds of their economy is stealing from this farm—just petty stuff, but that leads to bigger stuff. The really dangerous tsotsis come from Sole and Chabija townships. They come prepared for a proper dustup—sawn-off shotguns and machetes."

I shielded my eyes from the sun. "Those villagers look as if they have quite a well-established setup," I said.

"What?! They're pissing about with half an acre of millet and then whatever they can catch in the river. Anyway, why work when you can steal from me and then sit on your arse for the rest of the day? Just wait, though. Now, now I'll get my electric fence wired up and then hokoyo! Zap! One time, fried gondie."

K rubbed Dispatch's belly with his toe. "I can't turn away their kids, though. Their laaities come to my little school on the farm and I end up treating all of them at the clinic when they're sick. Mind you, the clinic is just for the ordinary things like malaria and coughs. If someone gets really sick, then I take them to the mission. Or if they get in a messy accident . . ." K licked his lower lip. "There was a woman here just the other day—when was it?" He frowned. "October, November time. It was before the rains, you know, when everything is so dry. Anyway this nanny was down there doing her washing and she got grabbed by a flattie. Just down there"—K pointed to the river below the village—"I was up at the office and Innocent, my cookboy, he comes running from the house and he's chemering, 'Bwana! Bwana! Crocodile!'

"And I come running after him and I hear this noise—Waaaaah! Waaaaah! The other nannies were on the bank tossing rocks at the flattie and screaming. Man! So I'm up here thinking, Do I get my gun or what? But I was scared of losing sight of her—you know, if it pulled her down, then what the hell do I do? And how was I going to shoot the flattie and miss the nanny? So I start yelling, man! I'm just screaming at Him, 'Father! Help me! Help me!' And I am running down to the river as fast as I can, picking up rocks and grabbing branches, and I bloody nearly fell into the river myself."

K was African in his storytelling, reliving the incident with dramatic gestures and loud shouting. The veins in his neck were standing out and he was sweating. He wiped his face with the back of his hand and then he went on more quietly. "And wouldn't you know, just as I get down there, the damn thing let her go. She was pretty shredded, though." K let this sink in for a moment before adding, "So I go wading in there, and my fucking hair must have been standing straight up, because the whole time I'm thinking there's a pissed-off flattie swimming around in here and he still wants his nosh. But what the hell am I going to do? The nanny was drowning. I had to go after her. I told the Lord, 'You keep that flattie away from me or I will scribble one of your own creatures.' And then I am in the current and I am just swimming. . . . I grab the nanny and she's just like"—K raked his nails up and down his arms—"it was like she had been chewed and digested and shat back into the water. I couldn't even tell if she was alive, but I hold on to her chin and I pull her to shore and there's blood everywhere. There's blood on the nanny and blood on me and blood in the water, and I'm sure every croc from here to Wasa Basa was on his way up to check it out.

"Anyway, I pick up the nanny and I run!" K laughed. "I must have made it from the riverbank to the pickup in about thirty seconds and the whole time I'm telling God, 'Don't let her die now. Please, God, don't let her die now.' But for all I know, she was already dead, because she was as gray as a bloody sheet. And I drove to the mission like a . . . what now? Bee-ba! Bee-ba," said K, laughing and imitating a siren. "Anyway, sure enough, she lived. When I brought her back from the mission—all stitched up from head to toe—I told them, 'You must thank the Father for giving you back your sister.' I said, 'Next time He might not be so kind.'"

As if in response to K's story, the river burped with barely submerged life and there was a sudden splash. The air hummed with insects and with the anticipation of more rain, and as we sat there, the drops began to fall, silver beads that speckled the river and drew a curtain of wet around us. The dogs slunk onto the veranda and the cat streaked for the kitchen. We could hear the workers shouting to one another as they ran for shelter. The rain intensified and we joined the dogs, pulling up chairs until our knees pressed together in the tight patch of dry afforded by the shallow breadth of roof. Our sense of isolation was complete.

I tried to picture K elsewhere and failed. Like the African earth itself, he seemed organic and supernatural all at the same time, romantic and brutish, a man who was both savior and murderously dangerous. And he was much, much more complicated than the stereotypes it was so tempting to use to describe him. Seeing him on this farm, I couldn't decide if the man had shaped the land or the other way around.

"How did you find this place?" I asked.

K stroked one of the dogs and said nothing for a long time and then, when he did speak, his voice was almost unbearable to hear. His resigned sadness, as real and tangible as humidity, wrapped itself around my shoulders, and I felt ruined with pity. "It's lekker, isn't it?" he said.

"Beautiful," I agreed.

"Sometimes," said K, "when I am lying in bed at night and thinking about how I got here, I can only say that it must have been God's plan from the start. Every step of my life has been one step closer to this." K shrugged, as if he was helpless to prevent the seclusion and remoteness and as if his heart had finally broken. He seemed to me then to be a man not so much wallowing in his good fortune, but accepting his inevitable punishment.

"You know"—K cleared his throat—"I was called up when I was seventeen. I was an appy at a workshop in Que Que when I got my papers. I wanted to be a welder." He sighed. "See? I started off with good intentions. Then . . . well, I was called up into the regulars and the first week in camp I was slow getting out of bed one morning, so the sergeant—some bullying prick—

comes up to me and boots me as hard as he can in the small of the back. He told me, 'Get up, soldier!'

"Ja, well I learned to defend myself in boarding school, so man . . . I didn't mess around. In about three seconds I had the sarge with my hand around his neck, pinned half a meter off the floor to the barracks door. I knew right then that if I stayed in the regulars I'd end up killing someone on the wrong side— I mean on our own side: some idiot who didn't have a clue and who thought he could bully me just because he had a stripe on his shoulder and I didn't.

"What you have to understand is that I grew up in the shateen, I grew up with a gun, I grew up with the gondies, I grew up fighting. The war was not a mission for me. It was like I'd done all my life except instead of hunting game, I was hunting gooks."

The early afternoon had turned a mellow golden color. The rain swallowed itself back up into the clouds. The lemon-colored sun sank down and bulged in the high western sky. The land beyond the river looked as if it was steaming gently.

"And I could hunt gooks better than anyone because I could think like one. When I was a laaitie, my folks had a farm in Kalamo, in southwestern Zambia. It was still Northern Rhodesia in those days. I must have been about four when my grandfather took me with him herding cattle from Munz to Kaleni. I walked with the munts the whole way—a couple of hundred kilometers—while the old boy drove. At night, the old man camped in a tent, and I slept with the cattle boys around the fire. And they showed me how to think like a munt, and how to track—even after cows have trampled the shateen down to a toothpick, they showed me how to pick up traces of spoor—and they showed me to hunt, just little things, like mice and rabbits." K paused. "If you can track a rat, you can sure as shit track a person. So," continued K, "I joined the RLI."

"Did they check under your fingernails to make sure you were white?"

K laughed. "No, but they sent me into the shateen with a savage sergeant to see if I could survive for three weeks in the bush with that arsehole. Which I could. Then they gave me a gun to see if I could hit a target. Which I could. Then they did everything they could think of to kill me for months and months, and when I was still alive at the end of it, they said, 'Congratulations.' They gave me a bazooka and said, 'Go forth and scribble.' So I phoned up my dad and I told him I was in Thirteen Troop and he said to me, 'If you want to fuck up your life, go ahead.'" The muscles in the back of K's jaw hopped. "But"—he let his breath out—"it was too late by then. I was in."

"Do you regret it?"

K looked at me for a long time, considering the question. "Not like you'd expect," he said at last. "My whole life would have been different if it hadn't been for the war so . . . In some ways, the war years were the best of my life. Those boys that I fought with—there were four of us in a troop, that's it . . . man, I knew them better than I knew myself. You walk into the shateen with three strangers and a month later you walk out with ous that you've had to trust with your life and who have trusted you with their lives and you know them so well. You've seen them shit themselves with fright, you've cried with them, you've laughed a lot. . . ." K looked out at the river and went quiet. Then he said, "Always, forever after"—K crossed his fingers and held up his hand to show me—"you will not forget them. Even the Yanks from Vietnam and those crazy buggers from Northern Ireland, and the Frogs and the Kiwis. . . . We were all in it together, it didn't matter where you came from. And I learned a lot from those ous. By the end of the war, I could say 'fuck you,' 'fuck me,' and 'fuck off' in four different languages." K laughed and then he said, "Unless you've licked the arse end of the world with a man, you can't know what it's like to have that kind of relationship with someone. It's closer than family. And that's why it hurt. . . ." K looked away and shook his head; when he spoke again, his voice was strangled with tears: "The guy lying in the wank-sack next to you might have been a jerk in the real world, but out there in the shateen. . . . We all knew that none of us were angels, but we covered for each other. We were so close with each other that . . . it was like we spoke a different language—our own language."

K sighed and his shoulders sagged. "There was this one ou— my best friend, you could say he was my Stone China. He was the guy that was always right there, by my side for five years. After the war he was nailed by some gondies in Jo'burg. They jumped him at a red light and they blallered his skop and stole his car. He was completely spazzed out for months but when he got out of hospital I told him he must come and live with us, with me and my wife. So he came and lived with us because he wasn't square—he couldn't look after himself, he couldn't really talk, his brain was like sadza. But, of course, I took care of him under my own roof. I told my wife, 'Treat him as if he were your own brother.'" K paused. "And then I come to find the bloody cripple's screwing my wife." K made a choking noise that might have been a laugh. "Ja, that's how he thanked me for taking care of him for three years. That's how he treated his best friend."

The hippos surfaced and shouted their objection into the lowering sun.

"So that was the marriage over, more or less. It had been on the rocks for a while, but that was the final straw. Me, I decided, 'Screw this.'

"I told the ex: 'You take everything, my girl. The house, the garden, the car, the business. Me, I am heading into the bush.'

"I got sod all except a boat. So that year, at the end of the rains, I hopped in the boat and I started at the top of the gorge and I floated down these rivers every chance I got for two years. And one day, I was coming along here"—K pointed upstream—

"and I look up on the shore, and there's a lekker crop of turbo cabbage." K put an imaginary joint to his lips and sucked in a deep lungful of air. "I pulled my boat over and I go looking to see whose weed it is. But there's no one here. Not a soul. It's just shateen for miles and bloody miles. The dagga was wild, self-cultivated. But man! I dried some and smoked it and the stuff almost blew my wig off. Anyway, the cabbage wasn't the point. It was this land.

"I spent two nights here that first time, just sleeping on the ground, under the stars. Right here under this tree, I cleared the damn jesse scrub and buffalo bean and slept right here. All night, I kept asking the Almighty, 'Is this what You want for me?' And all day I walked, deeper and deeper into the shateen and I just kept seeing that it was more and more beautiful and more and more wild.

"Then the next month I found the chief having a few drinks with Alex and Marie down at Malidadi and he agreed to have discussions with me and after a few months he granted me the land. Have you met him? Old Chief Chabija."

I nodded. The chief was well respected from Sole to Kariwa, ruthlessly stubborn and notoriously fair. (He rejected land claims by anyone who arrived at his boma carrying bribes, but nevertheless expected gifts from his visitors commensurate with their means. The difference between a bribe and a gift seemed to depend on the chief's assessment of the gift-giver.) Anyone requesting land from the chief—my parents included—could expect both arbitrary and thorough inspections, as well as a rigorous trial period during which the chief ensured the land was being developed as promised and that jobs were going to his people, and not to workers from other provinces.

K said, "Half his relatives work here now, so I'm long Chinas with the chief."

The sun caught the tip of the escarpment and flooded the lower western sky with a golden thread. A young man clad in a camouflage-patterned tank top and green trousers came to the gate and beat the gong.

K put his hand out to stay the dogs. "Come!" he told the man.

The young man came down to the veranda. "I am Innocent," he announced.

"Bo," I said, shaking his hand.

Innocent took the tea tray to the kitchen and began to retrieve clothes from the washing line. I glanced at my watch and said that I thought it was time I started to head home.

K stood up. "But there's something I want to show you first."

"Perhaps another time," I suggested. "I have a long walk back to the road."

"No, no. You don't need to leave right now. You're in no hurry. I'll drive you home. I'll drive quickly," said K. "Did you have enough tea? Enough to eat?"

"Plenty, thank you."

"Come now," ordered K. He led me away from the veranda and garden, through the farmyard, and cut sharply toward the bend in the river, on a path cleared through the bush. Vervet monkeys clattered overhead and openbill storks stood sentry in the top reaches of a winter thorn tree. Suddenly, the bush opened up into an expanse of rain-misted lawn. A half-built redbrick house in the middle of a freshly planted lawn stood watch over the river, facing the square head of a mountain on the far bank.

"That," said K, pointing across the river, "is Peace Mountain."

I had seen the mountain before from the tarmac road. It is a distinctive wedge-shaped rise of land with a wide band of cliffs at its neck. "I didn't know it had a name," I said.

"It didn't," said K. "I named it." His voice thickened. "I climbed it last year. I got caught on a cliff. I just had to hang there and wait for the Almighty to tell me what to do. If it hadn't been for Him . . . It took me until well after dark to get down, just praying to Him to guide me as I went." K demonstrated a massive bowl of a hand. "You have to remember that He holds each and every one of us right there, right in the palm of His hand."

"Luckily," I said.

K frowned. "Come," he said, leading me up to the house. It stood stubbornly in the middle of the lawn, the reverse of a ruin (something being built up against the press of the Sole Valley sun, instead of the more usual experience of something crumbling and melting back into the ground).

"And this," said K as he stepped into the roofless house, "is where we'll live one day. I'll finish building it soon. I have to get the farm going a bit more first, though. But what do you think?"

I wondered who "we" was, but I didn't ask. Instead I said, "It's lovely."

"Look," said K, "it's all set up for books. Shelves here, and here. Maybe you could put ornaments on this shelf. This is the kitchen. See? A view of the mountain out the window." He turned to me and I can describe the look on his face only as transported. "I don't think," he said, "that God is going to have me make this journey alone. He will send me a woman when the time is right."

A blue-headed lizard scampered up the wall where the larder shelves would be one day and one of the dogs darted after it, barely catching the end of its tail, which sloughed off and wiggled hysterically on the cement-dusted floor.

"She'll have to be a very special woman," said K, softly and looking at me.

"Yes," I said.

And then, maybe it was a trick of the rain-softened light, but I saw K's face fold with such exquisite torment that my heart turned over for him.

He said, "There's been so much destruction. But I've learned so much now. I've really learned about love." K's lips grew fleshy. "I would nurture a woman. She would be the head of the family now. I wouldn't have to dominate her. I would put everyone else first. I would come last in the family. This is the order: first God, then my wife, then my children, the dogs, the servants. . . . I would be last. I just want to share this"—he gestured to the house, the garden, the slow-churning river—"with someone."

I looked away from the house and saw that three fishermen had paddled their canoes around the bend in the river. The evening had brought a kind of careless, extravagant beauty to the world. The sky was rinsed various shades of blue and pink and was scattered with ripped, high clouds. The sun, catching itself in the trees on the far bank, bled red and gold across the water. Peace Mountain and the distant escarpment were softened in a dying light. From the village opposite K's farm, blue clouds of smoke from cooking fires tugged into the evening sky. It was the time of day when the confusion of color, the churn of cooler air supplanting the heat of the day, the miracle of the journeying river—everything about being alive—seemed more improbable and fleeting and precious than usual.

The Left Behind

Sole Valley village

THE ROAD FROM the boundary of K's farm to the tarmac had not been improved by the day's rain. The bridge over the gorge had been repaired, but there were several other sections of the road that had given way and were torn in sharp, washed-away gullies. K drove fast and determinedly and although the car sometimes slipped and spun, we managed somehow to stay on track and forge the streams that tumbled brown and frothy in their new, temporary capacity as rivers.

As we dipped into warm pockets of air that had sunken into dambos and vleis, the air expanded with the comforting smell of the potato bush and there was a ricochet of insects shrilling.

We flashed past huts that, in the dim light, had lost their shabby air of poverty and had taken on instead the aura of cozy domesticity. Indistinct shapes huddled over cooking fires, the occasional snatches of life (a child crying, a man shouting, a woman's high voice calling out) tumbled through the air at us.

"I like you," said K suddenly.

I startled and hesitated before I said, "I like you too."

"I don't like most people," K said. "Most wazungu."

"No."

"I find I don't trust people. It's hard to trust someone who hasn't looked up the wrong end of a barrel. You know?"

"I don't make a habit of looking up guns' snouts," I admitted.

K persisted. "Ja, how do you know what someone is made of until you've broken cover with them at exactly the same time?"

"But I haven't broken cover with you," I pointed out.

"No, but you're a woman," said K, as if that exempted me.

"Yes," I agreed, knowing it didn't.

K drove in silence for a bit longer. The road ahead—its surface magnified in the headlights—told a vivid story of everything that had walked or run or driven over it since the rain had stopped. Bicycle tracks snaked; goat hooves poked sharp dents; flat feet padded; cows left deep grooves; donkeys were daintier and tripping.

"Man," said K, "every time I drive through here I think of Mozambique. This patch of bush just here is exactly like Mozambique. See how it is—this flat sandy mopane with the scrub on the side and these piles from old anthills? It's just like in Moz." Then he shuddered and added, "I'm going to give myself spooks, talking about the war all day."

"Don't you usually talk about it?"

K said, "I don't usually talk about *anything*. I don't have anyone *to* talk to except the gondies. . . . And you know how it is to talk to these guys? I love these munts, I really do, but . . . I don't really talk to them. I mean, we talk about the farm and the river and the weather and money—we're always talking about their blerry money problems—and about their indabas in the village. . . . They tell me all their hunna-hunna about who's bonking whose wife and who is beating up who and they want me to fine the offenders and tell them who is right and who is wrong, but I can't tell them about the ex or about myself or about, you know . . . about my life. About the war. If I told Michael what I told you today he'd shit himself. Don't you think? He'd shit himself."

"Probably not," I said.

K was quiet for a few minutes and then said, "Ja, well, in any case, it's true that I'd rather sit and talk to a fisherman on the Chabija all day about tiger fish and bream and his bloody millet crop than try and spend one afternoon chatting to a honky about his shallow crap. No . . . maybe it's just that this hondo stuff shouldn't be spoken at all. Not to a gondie or to you or to anyone."

And then the pickup gave a jolting buck and we were hiccuped out onto the tarmac. A black, curling ribbon of shiny highway, connecting the fragments of Zambia that fall on this side of the escarpment to the city of Lusaka. As we turned up the dirt road toward my parents' camp, the headlamps swung briefly against Sole's candlelit brothels and caught the stunned eyes of drunks on the verandas of the throbbing taverns.

"You must stay for a drink when we get to the camp," I told K.

"No, I should get home," said K. "I have a busy day tomorrow. Anyway, I don't drink anymore."

"I think I knew that."

"Who told you?"

"It was an international news flash when you stopped."

K laughed. "Ja, it should have been. I used to drink. Mai we, I used to drink!"

Suddenly, a man riding a bike with a woman balanced across his handlebars came reeling out of the village, wobbled in front of the pickup for a few swollen seconds, and then veered out of the way. K spun the steering wheel and the pickup juddered off the road, where it cruised along at a terrifying angle before regaining four wheels.

K carried on talking as if nothing had happened. "All of us guys, you'll find we drink in binges. Three weeks sober and then a week of being absolutely blallered. Maybe a bottle of vodka and a dozen beers in a night. It's what we learned in the war."

I glanced behind us and the man and the woman were toiling on through the mud, quite matter-of-factly, their faces reflected red in the tail lights of the pickup.

"You're in the shateen for three weeks straight," K was saying, "and then you're back in camp for a week and you spend the first three days trying to forget the last three weeks and the next three days trying not to think about the next three weeks and one night with an almighty hangover and then you're back in the shateen." K shook his head. "Voddies and Coke was my drink," he said. "But my hangovers! And my demons! One night about two years after the war I was in a hotel room with the ex, and you know those ceiling fans with a toggle on the end of a string to switch the thing on and off, ja? Well, in my sleep, I guess, I could hear the fan—thuka, thuka, thuka—and the toggle—tinka, tinka, tinka—and in my alcoholic state I thought it was a helicopter coming to chaya me. Man, I woke up and I was screaming and leaping around the bed and donnering that fan with a pillow and there were feathers flying everywhere and the ex was screaming at me. But I honestly thought I was under attack, which was bull if you think about it because in real life, it was *us* with the choppers and the gooks getting stonked with those K-cars."

K drove in silence for a moment. Then he said, "Thank God— I thank the Almighty—that I stopped the old elbow-lifting exercises because those other boys . . . binge? Ja, that's how they still operate. They work like dogs for three weeks and then they soup it up for a solid week. That's how we got through the war. That's how we learned to get through real life."

K paused and then he said, "I can't blame them though. You know, if I didn't believe in the Heavenly Father, I think I might have scribbled myself by now, either by accident or on purpose. Because what's the point of life? Do you know what the point of life is?"

"No," I said, "I haven't figured it out yet."

"I'll tell you," said K. "Unless you have been saved by Jesus, life is just the few seconds you have before death. That's it. Over and out . . . Without Jesus as your savior, that's all life is. . . . And doing everything you can to forget that you're going to snuff it shortly is your single mission in life." K turned to me in the darkness. "Do you know how I know this?"

"No," I said.

K was speaking with a preaching voice, a voice that was supposed to reach into the dark, cool corners of a church. "We were all lost after the war," he told me. "I reckon those of us who stopped dopping and sucking cabbage, we started to feel . . . shit! I mean, we actually started to think about what had happened to us because—you know—we had sobered up. How come we aren't dead? Where are we? Why are we here? What are we doing? We went from this incredible structure, this incredible focus and sense of purpose . . . You were either in, or out. Alive or dead. And then it was over and . . . All of a sardine, we had to figure it out by ourselves and what we found is that nothing seemed to matter about the outside world. It was all pointless. How much can it matter what kind of car you drive? How can it matter what you eat, I mean as long as you have enough to eat? How much can it matter what you wear? When you get down to it, what can matter more than being alive? But then what? You're alive and then . . . what?"

All around us the rinsed air and sky and world seemed endlessly black, as if you could plunge into it in any direction and fall forever. A nightjar exploded up from in front of the headlights and seemed to hang there for an age before dipping into the night. By now, we had turned off the mud-rutted road that leads from Sole to Malidadi and onto the high gravel spine of driveway that leads through the mopane pan to Mum and Dad's camp. Only a few days ago an army of bullfrogs had frolicked and seethed here. Now the shallow lake rippled out on either side of the track, vast and anonymous and almost silent.

"What do you see when you look in the mirror?" K asked suddenly. "Do you see yourself?"

"Yes."

"But yourself isn't a thing. How can you see something that isn't there? You are just meat and bones. That's what you should see. Flesh and blood, that's all. And all flesh and blood is . . . Do you want to know what flesh and blood is?" K waited. "You and me and every other person on this earth—we're all just a bloody corpse waiting to happen. I don't care how good-looking you think you are. How successful you believe you are. Your body is still just a corpse-in-waiting."

By now we were back at the fish camp. I could see the pale yellow light of bare bulb that swung from the kitchen roof from under the arch. I could see Mum's bed, through the window of her room, shrouded with a mosquito net. The signature tune of the BBC World Service sang jauntily out to us. K kept the engine running and his face glowed green in the reflected light from the dashboard. The engine ticked in the heat.

I took a deep breath. "This corpse-in-waiting could do with a drink," I said.

K said, "Man, I'm sorry. I'd have stopped at Harry's Bar if I'd known you were so desperate."

"That's okay," I said. "I'm fine, really. Thank you for . . . every-thing."

K stared straight ahead. "It was my pleasure," he said stiffly.

And then, as I was turning to open the car door, K suddenly launched across the cab and planted a hot kiss on my cheek. "Good-bye," he said. And before I had properly closed the door, he was driving away.

The Leftovers

Bobo

AFTER I MET K, there were odd chunks of time when I did not think of him at all. And then there were vast stretches of nights when I woke so full of him that I wondered if I had dreamed him into life by accident. My accident. My fault. It was as if the hot Sole soil had met the unaccustomed flush of that extraordinary rain and out of the violence of this encounter, K had been hallucinated into life as my *idea*. He had been grafted into reality in the hothouse of my imagination. K the idea. Which is so much worse than K the real person from whom I could walk away.

K was a fantasy or a nightmare. He was an act of God. Or of

Evil. Or of both. K was shell-shocked. K was explosive. K was given to us as a solution, or as a punishment. Depending on whose side you were on. The world was both less equivocal and much more confusing with him in my mind. There was no "warm," no "gray," no "maybe." It was "hot or cold," "black or white," "yes or no."

Are you in or out?

In late December I went home to my husband and to my children and to the post-Christmas chaos of a resort town, but instead of feeling glad to be back, I was dislocated and depressed. It should not be physically possible to get from the banks of the Pepani River to Wyoming in less than two days, because mentally and emotionally it is impossible. The shock is too much, the contrast too raw. We should sail or swim or walk from Africa, letting bits of her drop out of us, and gradually, in this way, assimilate the excesses and liberties of the States in tiny, incremental sips, maybe touring up through South America and Mexico before trying to stomach the land of the Free and the Brave.

Because now the real, wonderful world around me—the place where we had decided to live with our children, because it had seemed like an acceptable compromise between my Zambia and my husband's America—felt suddenly pointless and trivial and almost insultingly frivolous. The shops were crappy with a Christmas hangover, too loud and brash. Everything was 50 percent off. There was nothing challenging about being here, at least not on the surface. The new year's party I attended was bloated with people complaining about the weight they had put on over Christmas. I feigned malaria and went home to bed for a week.

It wasn't that I didn't want to join in the innocent, deluded self-congratulation that goes with living in such a fat, sweet country. I did. But I couldn't. And confining myself to the house didn't help. Now I felt like a trespasser in my own home with all its factory-load of gadgets and machines and the ease of the push-button life I was living. And, uninvited, K strolled around in the back of my head and talked his loneliness out of himself and straight into me and would not let me rest and by the end of this, there were pieces of me and pieces of him and pieces of our history that were barbed together in a tangle in my head and I couldn't shake the feeling that in some inevitable way, I was responsible for K. And he for me.

Then gradually the winter seeped into spring and I resumed the habits of entitlement that most of us don't even know we have. And K's imaginary voice—which had been an almost continuous presence through the cold weather—melted into an only occasional intrusion. I drank coffee at the café on the creek without imagining K asking me how I could pay three times the average Zambian's daily salary for the privilege; I ate sun-dried tomatoes and wild mushrooms drizzled with extra-virgin olive oil and the ghost of K didn't appear to tell me that you were either a virgin, or not, but you couldn't be extra-virgin. And I disentangled myself from my history, one sticky thread at a time, until I was completely, happily reestablished as a Wyoming mother. I started to take the ease for granted.

Then in late August, I woke up one night into the brittle light of a Rocky Mountain full moon. I had been crow-dropped and caught by the silly bell-bottoms again. I lay in bed feeling rigid and my skin burned with that old terrorist-under-the-bed feeling. The moon had set the world alight in a pale, cold fire of silver. The fir tree outside our bedroom window gleamed blue and rapped an urgent tattoo against the glass. I got out of bed (feet prickling) and went through to the kids' room. They were both asleep, their faces turned up to the light that shattered through their window. I sat on the edge of their beds and kissed them both, hungry for the kind of peace they usually instilled in me. My daughter turned over and hugged her blanket to her belly. My son muttered. It felt as if I was imparting disquiet into my children, as if my embrace were poisoned.

I went through to the kitchen—feeling exiled by who I was—and made some tea and sat on the sofa with a blanket over my knees. It was the time of night that precedes dawn and is without perspective or reason. It was the hour when regret and fear overwhelm hope and courage and when all that is ugly in us is magnified and when we are most panic-stricken by what we have lost, and what we have almost lost, and what we fear we might lose.

Then I remembered an incident from when I was five or six (not yet at boarding school). I remembered waking up into the impenetrable blackness of an African night; we had no electricity and I, who had set my sheets on fire looking under the bed for terrorists, had been banned from touching anything to do with fire and, as extra insurance, all matches and candles had been confiscated from beneath my pillow and from under the mattress where I had been stashing them for months. I lay there in the dark as long as I could stand it and then I exploded with a hissing whisper, "Vanessa! Wake up!"

My sister, who was three years older than me, groaned, "What?"

"Light your candle! There's a terrorist under my bed."

"No there isn't. Go back to sleep."

"There is!"

"Not."

"Is."

And Vanessa, sensing that this might go on until morning, replied (by way of not-much-comfort), "Just think of all the poor terrorists who are lying awake right now, afraid to go to sleep in case they have *you* under their beds."

God Is Not My Messenger

Sole store

IN OCTOBER, I flew from Wyoming to Zimbabwe to write a story for an English newspaper about the political crisis there—the country's president, Robert Mugabe, and his cronies had turned on their own people in a vicious reversal of intention, eating the power bestowed on them and tumorous with the excess of it. At the end of my trip, demoralized by the corruption and violence I had witnessed, I bought a bus ticket from Harare to Sole with the intention of spending a few nights with Mum and Dad before returning to the States.

My fellow bus travelers included several Zimbabweans who were trying to look as if they always brought the kitchen sink with them when they came on "holiday" to Zambia but whose shaking hands and sweating faces at the police roadblocks gave them away as political refugees. There were smugglers from the Democratic Republic of the Congo with little glassy rocks for sale in their shirt pockets (diamonds, or they were offered as diamonds to me, who couldn't remember if you were supposed to bite them or scratch glass with them to see if they were real). There was a Zambian woman who casually told me that she was a prostitute. There were three Mozambican traders with baskets of dried fish, bottles of cooking oil, and bolts of cloth. They sat in the back of the bus like gate-crashers, with the surreptitious, suspicious air of people who have been used to groveling at the depths of what the world has to offer and have suddenly and unexpectedly found their fortunes rising, but who have seen enough of the capriciousness of fate to expect their luck to dry up at any moment.

By the time we had broken down once, lost luggage once (the rope holding everyone's belongings to the roof had snapped), and made numerous stops for one or another of the passengers to crouch behind a bush or tree, it was late afternoon. By then, the heat from the day had gathered itself together for a final assault on the earth and was pounding onto the road, which shuddered in a series of dislocated heat waves before us, and onto the land on either side of the road and into the bus. As we crawled off the escarpment at Mkuti and sank into the Pepani Valley, the dry air rushed up to meet us and we all opened our windows as wide as they would go and some of us drank beer, warm from the bottle. The prostitute passed around pieces of chicken, which, if it had ever been cold, was back up to oven temperature by now.

I'd forgotten how October eats at the landscape in the lowveldt. It is the most discouraging time of year: long enough after the last rains so that they are barely worth the ache of remembering and too far until the next rains to waste the energy on hope. All signs of the memorable excesses of ten months ago had disappeared and it was hard to believe that the same valley could accommodate such disparate worlds. The sky was cloudless but stained wildfire yellow and the deep haze caught at the heat waves. Goats and donkeys stood with their backs to the sun and closed their eyes, panting (visibly rocking with every labored breath). The ground around the villages was exposed, brick hard and grazed clean of vegetation.

The Goba people say October is Gumiguru, meaning "month of the big ten"; November is the infinitely more hopeful Mbuzdi, meaning "month of goat fertility," but October is big and ominous and obscurely ten. The Goba wisely avoid holding wedding and initiation ceremonies in October. White locals know it as suicide month. The Nyanja call it Mwenzi wa zuma, meaning "month of the sun." They also call it Kusi piya (from kusi piya weka, "to kill yourself"). It is not a month to be toyed with.

Dad was waiting at the border for me. He was sitting on the front of the pickup, feet hooked over the front bumper, in the shade of a mango tree. He was smoking his pipe and staring placidly through the anarchic tumult of money traders (flapping fists of money at him, as if they had caught wild birds and were trying to sell them) and the drunks who lurched occasionally into the street from nearby taverns, blinked with dismay at the unremitting sun, and then tottered back into the humid gloom of the bars. Dad smiled and waved when he saw me stagger through the gates, laden with computer, backpack, and baskets of gifts acquired at the Harare market.

"Hello, Bobo," he said. "Manage to stay out of the clanger?"

I kissed him. "Bit bloody scary, though," I said, looking back over the river to Zimbabwe, which, from the safety of here, looked deadened and stultified by the terrific heat and too dazed for any hope of an uprising. Which is what it needed. Either that, or a variation on a medieval theme. In those years, to ensure the continuing prosperity of the land, the Shona people of the great Munhumutapa empire had not allowed their Mambo to grow old. Instead, the Mambo was ritually slain after four years and an unfortunate replacement selected.

"Other than that, okay?" asked Dad.

I nodded. "Fine. Thanks for coming to fetch me."

"Mum wouldn't let me make you walk to the farm," said Dad. "Not since the last bloke snuffed it."

"Who snuffed it?"

"Some Pom from Lusaka wanted to be shown around the farm a couple of weeks ago, so I took him out for a little walk and he did a heels-up."

"Completely?"

"Fell off his perch."

"What do you mean by 'a little walk'?"

"Just around the farm."

"God, Dad."

"Heat exhaustion or some bloody thing." Dad heaved my suitcase into the back.

"Poor man."

"He wasn't very talkative to begin with and then he went completely quiet."

"Dad!"

"Mum went to the funeral," said Dad defensively.

"I suppose that's something," I said.

"I told her not to look conspicuous but she still dressed like a bloody bullfighter, wore a hat that could start a rebellion, and apparently sat as close as she could get to the coffin without falling into it."

"Ha."

Dad looked over at me and allowed himself a little laugh.

THE FIRST TWO DAYS passed quietly. Mum and Dad were busy on the farm all morning (fish, if nothing else, seem to breed and grow extravagantly in October) and I stayed up at the camp pretending to write while they were gone. Everything felt entangled by the heat, as if it were able to throw out limb-snagging webs that caught at our ankles, our arms, and even our tongues, making us all slower-moving than usual and more languid of speech.

We woke very early—mashambanzou, the Goba say, "when the elephants wash"—to take advantage of what little respite from the sun the night might have given us (the earth swallowed heat all day and regurgitated it all night). But by midmorning, when the buffalo beans tossed up stinging hairs from their fruit into the air—hairs that found skin and burrowed into flesh with burning insistence—all activity on the farm came to a halt. Everyone found refuge in the damp shade of the banana plantation, or in the cool gloom of a hut, and slept off the poisonous part of the day, awaking in late afternoon feeling tongue-swollen and bleary. Then, we drank tea and worked for another two or three hours, until sundown approached.

In the evenings—marirangwe, the Goba say, "when the leopard calls out"—we took cold beers down to the banks of the river and watched the sky turn from a sun-wrecked wash of pale yellow-blue to a vivid display of reds and yellows and lurid, clashing streaks of purple. Doves called and trilled prettily to one another from the fig trees, crickets buzzed in the whispering dry grass, and, from the villages, an intermittent volley of dog barks and the wails of children shattered the air. Hippos, pink and gray humps scattered like rocks off the edges of eddies, occasionally surfaced under a spray of water and honked a warning at the shadowy dugout canoes that skimmed past them.

Late on the afternoon of the third day, after Mum and Dad had gone down to the tanks to admire a fresh crop of fingerlings, K appeared, looming under the arch at the top of the camp as he had the first time I had met him, and blocking out the sun, which spread indistinctly in a pale explosion behind a mile-thick choke of dust and wood smoke.

"Hi." I shaded my eyes against the beat of light.

"Huzzit?" K took the steps that lead down from the archway to the tamarind tree in his characteristically greedy gulps. "I heard you had come home," he said, pulling up a camp chair next to me and pouring himself a cup of tea, draining the pot.

"Should I brew some fresh?"

K swallowed down the tea and said, "Please." He followed me into the kitchen. "You've been okay?" he asked.

This time, when I lit a match, the firewood was parchment dry and caught easily onto the flame. I put the kettle over the hottest part of the fire. "Ja, I've been fine."

The little dogs—those that had not gone with Mum and Dad to stare down into tanks and tanks of identical fish babies—had barely lifted their heads at K's arrival. Now a couple of them thumped their tails in greeting and K bent down to fondle their ears. They lay in panting crescent-shaped heaps across the relatively cool kitchen floor, miniature lakes of saliva forming in silver pools below their mouths.

When the water boiled, splattering and hissing and adding to the general atmosphere of hellish heat, I poured it onto the small pile of tea leaves in the enamel pot and set the tea tray with a jug of milk and two clean cups.

"Here," said K, "let me take that for you."

We went back under the tamarind tree. K put the tray down

on the picnic table and then sat down next to me. I poured the tea and handed K a cup.

"How long are you here for?" he asked.

"A couple more days," I said.

"How are things in the States?"

"Fine."

"The kids and Charlie?"

"Well."

"Cheers."

We sipped our tea. A redchested cuckoo predicted, without any basis for her optimism, "It will rain! It will rain!"

"What are you working on?" asked K, looking at the computer and the sliding avalanche of notes and tapes.

"A newspaper article," I said.

"Is it going all right?"

"Not really." I lit a cigarette. "I'm trying to make sense of the mess in Zimbabwe in twelve hundred words."

K let this sink in for a moment and then he gave such a guffawing laugh that he sprayed tea over the table and then I started to laugh too. I slammed the lid of my computer shut, losing all unsaved work in one careless gesture, and said, "Oh God, how arrogant. You're right. Crazy to even try."

"No," said K earnestly, "you're not crazy to try. Sorry for laughing." He made an attempt at a straight face. "Sorry," he apologized, laughing again and covering his mouth with his hand. Then we were both laughing more than the comment had any right to.

"How's the farm?" I asked, when I had recovered my breath.

"Going strong."

I smiled at K. He smiled back. We drank tea. The heat sighed up from the earth and curled around my neck. I waved my cigarette smoke toward some flies that had settled on the edge of the milk jug. "It's warm, isn't it?"

K nodded. "I'm glad I'm not a gorilla." He showed me his hairless arms and legs. "When I played underwater hockey for Zimbabwe the ous used to tease me that I shaved."

"Under what?"

"Underwater hockey. I was on the national team for Zim."

"What's that?"

"It's hockey you play under water," said K. "On the bottom of the pool. You have little sticks and a puck. In Europe they play it in big pools with glass sides."

"You're kidding."

"I'm not. I was also on the Zim spearfishing team. We went to Turkey for a tournament." K laughed. "You should have seen! All the other teams had boats and radar and wet suits and there were us Zimbos with our flippers and snorkels and we had to smear ourselves with Vaseline so we didn't freeze. So we go paddling off the beach—and all the other teams are way out there, in the middle of the sea, diving off their fancy rigs—and start hunting for fish and I am swimming along and a bloody turd goes bobbing past me. But there was a huge fish chasing the turd, so I nailed that.

"Then I noticed there was a pipe this big"—K made a huge circle with his arms—"and there was not just one turd, but hobo of shit pumping into the sea and there were maninge fish, and big ones too, right there. So I called the boys over and we took turns hopping into the sewer and pulling out these monsters, man. We were doing quite well by the end of the first day except then, the next day, we got a little sick of swimming in kak, so we swam out to sea to look for fish and we had a little incident with the Turkish navy."

"With the what?"

"Apparently we swam into no-go waters and the next thing you know there's a torpedo boat gunning straight for us and this idiot in a white Elvis sailor suit throwing a thrombie in gibberish. I couldn't understand a word he said, so then he pointed a gun at me, just to make himself clear."

"What did you do?"

"I told him to fuck off and stop pointing his gun at me."

"And did he?"

"No. And there was bugger all I could do about it." K shook his head. "I guess you could say I lost that round. I had to bareka, or he was going to chaya me." He sighed. "Man, I hate to lose." Then he took a deep breath and leaned forward. "I get that from my mother," he told me. "She was a cheeky one that. Incredibly determined. Half Greek and half South African— we used to say she was the Greek salad. You know, she was also an incredible athlete, my mom. Very competitive. She played hockey for South Africa."

"Under water?" I asked.

"No, field," said K. "When she was in her early twenties— right in the middle of her career as an athlete—she got polio. That was it, she was finished. She was a complete cripple. The doctors said she'd never walk again, but she was a stubborn woman. She could do anything she set her mind to. The doctor said she'd never have kids. She had three of us. Okay, she couldn't have us naturally. But still she had us. She could get pregnant normally, but then she had to have cesareans to get us out. In Rhodesia in the fifties, that was a mission, I'm telling you. But that's the kind of woman she was. She had absolutely no muscles left in her stomach. You must see photos of her— I'll show you a photo of her sometime—she was completely collapsed on the side." K held his hands out to the side as if cradling an enormous bulge of unrestrained stomach. "Her stomach went all the way out here and she was all tipping over sideways, but it never stopped her."

K lifted up his left leg with both his hands and let it drop. "That's how she used to drive. She used to have to pick up her leg and drop it on the clutch or the accelerator or the brake. She only had two speeds in the car, flat out, or stopped dead." K laughed. "People used to see her coming and they'd dive off the road." He shook his head. "Gondies flying into the ditches left and right. Everyone used to bail out when they saw the Old Lady coming their way. Oh man, I'm telling you"—K looked at me slyly to see if I was listening and smiled—"that's when we were living on the farm in Kaleni, here in Zambia. Northern Rhodesia in those days. I was at boarding school in Matabuka. Shit, I hated it. I was only happy when I came home and I used to take my gun and a bit of biltong and bread and head out into the shateen all day. That, I loved. I've always loved the bush.

"But school was another story." K shook his head. "The house-mistress gave me stripes my first day of school for insolence— I was five years old. You should have seen"—K held up a thick thumb—"welts this thick on my arse. The Old Lady was cross about that." K paused. "She went into the mistress's office on Monday morning and she told her, 'Beat the little bastard as much as you want. But I see welts on his rear again and you will regret the day you laid a finger on him.'"

And then K got quiet and when he spoke again, his voice had lost its joking tone. "You know we went through three of the Old Lady's wheelchairs. I used to tie them to the back of the tractor and take my sisters for rides over the tobacco fields. It was bloody funny until the wheels came off and then Mom would be furious and she'd say, 'Wait till your father comes home,' and then I'd shit myself, because Dad had a sjambok and Mom didn't mind if *he* left welts on our backsides."

K continued, "Anyway, after we'd scribbled all the wheel-chairs, Mom decided it was too expensive to keep buying the things for us to tear apart. So she taught herself to walk using crutches. She could get around okay, but if she fell down, she was finished. She had to lie there until someone came to help her. But she was also an incredibly proud woman—incredibly proud. If she fell down in the garden and the Old Man was out in the fields and my sisters and I were at school, she'd crawl, hand over hand, all day to get to the veranda rather than allow a gondie to lay a finger on her. That's how proud she was. But you know," said K, pressing his thumbs into the palms of his hands, "she had these huge knots in her tendons from holding on to the crutches. Her hands were like claws. So when I was fourteen— I was at high school in Que Que by then, in Rhodesia—the Old Lady went to have her tendons operated on in Bulawayo." K sighed. "She was forty-four years old and she died on the operating table."

"Oh God." I put my teacup down with a crash. "How awful."

K said, "The headmaster called me out of class. He said, 'Your mother's dead. You can take the weekend off.' So that was a Friday. I went on the train to Bulawayo for the funeral. I met the Old Man there, and my sisters. On Monday I was back at school."

"That's it?" I said.

"Ja," said K.

"You must have been devastated."

K shrugged. "Ja, ja. Of course. It was a mission. But it was worse for Dad. He was a shell after Mom died. That's when he left Zambia and moved to Rhodesia."

"You only had the weekend to get over your mom's death."

K nodded.

"Did you cry?"

"Not really," said K. "But all my hair fell out. Even on my head. I was so bloody cold that winter, I wore underrods on my head and the master gave me the cane because he thought I was trying to be clever. I wasn't. I showed him—'Sir, I'm bald. My bloody head's freezing'—but he still gave me stripes. Although it's grown back on my head now"—K rubbed his hand over his hair—"but nowhere else."

"How did your sisters cope?"

"Okay, I think."

"Do you see much of them?"

"On and off."

We drank tea in silence together for a while. The sun had fallen behind the escarpment and evening was starting to creep its way up from the river. "What are you doing tomorrow?" asked K suddenly.

I looked at the pile of notes, the computer, the spilling ashtray, and the pyramid of old teacups on the veranda. "I should really try to do something about this," I said.

"Take a break," he said. "Come out fishing with me."

"I can't stand fishing."

"Then you sit in the boat and I fish."

"I don't know," I said, feeling guilty already and looking at my computer again.

"Look, maybe a day away from it and you'll come up with something to write."

I hesitated.

"Come on. It's too hot to work anyway."

"Okay."

"We'll take your old man's rig."

So, the next day, just after breakfast, K arrived with fishing rods, a hat, a cooler, and a basket of food (fruit from his farm mostly, with some vegetarian samosas from the truck stop at the bottom of the escarpment). He smeared sunscreen on my nose, put a hat on my head, and hurried me down to the canal that cuts up from the Pepani River into the fish farm.

Dad's boat is an old and ordinary banana boat, a bit leaky from the time a hippo bit it when Dickie, my brother-in-law, was out fishing over new year's, but it works, more or less, and has the charmed river smells of mud, weed, fish, and sunscreen. The boat was loosely tied was in the middle of a canal. K scooped me into his arms and waded thigh-deep into the water and I closed my eyes and envisioned crocodiles, and then he deposited me on the cooler and pushed the boat out into the weak current.

Where the canal met the Pepani, the current grabbed the nose of the boat and we were flung out into the wide expanse of river. I kept a wary eye on the hippos, which K appeared to be ignoring, and we motored downstream into the bright glare of water that swirled ahead. K fished and I read, cringing from the sun under a wide hat and a towel. If I shut my eyes I felt suspended in a hot bubble of peace; the water licking the edge of the boat, the creak of the hull, the sounds of K fishing, the occasional eerie cry from the fish eagles.

We ate lunch pulled up on an island with our toes dug in the sandy beach, keeping half an eye on the boat, which was bellied up on a stretch of sand just downstream from us. I smoked a cigarette, waving it around my head to get rid of the flies, and K stripped down to his underpants and waded into the river.

"How do I start the boat when you get eaten by a croc?" I asked. The engine of Dad's boat, in common with almost everything mechanical on the fish farm, had quirks of temperament that required an intimate knowledge of the psychology of machines to operate.

K laughed (a smack of reflected sun caught his throat and face in profile and turned him black, like a cardboard cutout).

I said, "I wish you wouldn't."

"I do this all the time," he said.

"Why don't you save it for rescue missions?"

"Nah, I'll be okay. I'm too tough for a flattie anyway."

"I'll just write that on your tombstone, shall I?"

K waited until he was chest-deep in the water and then went under. I waited several seconds and then I got to my feet, feeling stupid with a rising panic. This is exactly how people are said to be taken. In half a minute or so, K will resurface, he will shout once for help, a crocodile's tail will arc out of the water sending silver droplets of water and red droplets of blood into the air, and that will be all I will ever hear from K again. I will yell, throw rocks, and call on God. But I will stop short of running into the river. Nevertheless, I will tell everyone at his funeral that I did my best to save him. Everyone will know that I am lying.

And then he came up for air close to the boat, squirting a mouthful of Pepani water into the sky above his face, like a living fountain. He waded to shore and shook himself dry and came and sat next to me. "Ja, ja. Refreshing, hey."

"I was having croc visions."

K laughed. "When my time's up, it's up. I reckon my fate is all written in God's Big Book and there's not a whole lot I can do to change the time and place and nature of my death." K bit the lid off a beer for me. "Here," he said, "keep your hair on and drink this. I'm going fishing."

I lay back on the warm sand and put my hat over my eyes. I could hear K's fishing line; a high whine as it buzzed over the water, a pause, and then—*plop*. I dozed off and when I woke up I found that K had made an umbrella for me out of a towel and four sticks. "The shade from the tree shifted," he explained, "I didn't want you getting sunburned."

"Thanks."

"I'll get the boat," said K, handing me the fishing rod and wading off into the river. I stared at him sleepily as he plowed through the water and returned towing the boat behind him. With his dark skin and tight metallic gray hair, he looked colossal and African, like Mwetsi, the first man in Shona mythology, who started life under the waters and ended murdered by his own sons when he grew ill from the poison of a snake bite.

K lifted me into the boat and said, "Should we drift for a while?"

"Why not?" I put my feet up on the cooler and lit a cigarette.

The boat nosed silently into the current and we were tugged

downstream. The sun was poised to sink behind the hills in Zimbabwe. A hatch of mosquitoes drifted out of the water and floated off in a tender swell of air, cool and slow, casually drifting to shore. A noisy clutch of ibises burst off an island. "Ha-de-da! Ha-de-da!" they mocked. Weaver bird nests hung over the water and their occupants swooped out of them and into riverside foliage. The world was held in a confusion of color; the sun, diffused through heat and haze, seemed to lick everything golden red and orange while darker blue shadows crouched under the fig trees and riverbanks.

"I asked God if you were the one," said K suddenly.

"What?" I dropped my cigarette into the bottom of the boat.

"I asked Him, 'Why do you send her to me if she is not the one?'"

I found the cigarette before it could roll into the greasy film of petrol, water, and oil in the back of the boat. "God, that was close," I said.

"What?"

"We nearly blew up." I drowned the remainder of the cigarette in a sludge of beer at the bottom of a bottle.

"Why did He send you, if you are not it?"

"But He didn't send me," I pointed out. "I came of my own accord. I came to see Mum and Dad."

"Ja, but then, why did He send them?"

"You're reading too much into this."

K was silent for a while and then he said softly, "Ja, maybe. Maybe."

The boat gurgled against a ruffle of current. A swoop of bats skated out from the trees and swerved across the top of the water following the flutter of night insects.

I said, "Don't worry. Someone will appear."

"Maybe. Maybe not. I guess I'm happy either way." But he didn't sound happy.

I lit another cigarette and kept my hand cupped around it this time.

It was the time of day that hurries too quickly past, those elusive, regrettably beautiful moments before night, which are shorter here than anywhere else I have been. The achingly tenuous evening teetered for a moment on the tip of the horizon and then was overcome by night and suddenly the business of returning back to shelter was paramount. It is the time of day the Goba call rubvunzavaeni, "when visitors ask for lodging."

K said, "The Good Book says, 'Thou shalt not yoke yourself to disbelievers.'"

"That's me," I said. "Disbelieving Thomas."

K smiled. "Ja."

"I think God also said something about not yoking yourself to married women."

K laughed. "No," he said. "He was right. You're not the one."

"Nope."

Then we drifted in companionable silence until the evening star appeared and pointed the way home.

"Time to go back," said K.

I took my place at the front of the boat (I was on the lookout for hippos and rocks that I now would not be able to see in any case). I said, "A priest from the Chimanimanis once told me God made Africa first, while He still had imagination and courage."

"Ja," K said. "Struze fact. Although how would I know? I've hardly seen the world. A swimming pool in Holland when we were playing underwater hockey and the arse end of a blinking sewer in Turkey about sum up my traveling experience."

I smiled.

"And South Africa a few times. And Mozambique," said K, lowering the propeller into the water. "I've traveled there a whole hobo."

"Have you been back there since the war?"

K said, "To Beira only. I've never been back to Tete. That's where the kak was during the hondo. Long kak in Tete."

I paused and then said, the words tumbling from my lips before I had a chance to catch the thought that preceded them, "What if we went back? You and me."

"What?"

"To Mozambique."

"Why the hell would you want to go to Moz?"

"I could write about it and you could get over your spooks."

"Write about what?"

"I don't know. You? The war?"

"No ways, man. You want me to end up in Ingutchini?"

K started the engine and curled the boat up toward Mum and Dad's camp, taking us back over our own wake and spinning up quickly so that my feet, dangling over the edge of the water, were lifted high above the surface and I was only occasionally sprayed with stray droplets.

Just before the boat nosed into the cutting, K suddenly shouted to me, "Okay."

"What?" I shouted back.

"I'll go."

The nose of the boat caught an eddy and was spat back into the current so that I had to lean to one side to avoid getting tipped off the end of the boat.

"I'll go to Mozzy with you."

Oh God, Pandora, I thought. What have you done?

K cut the engine and we thumped into the damp bank. I jumped to shore with the rope and tied the boat.

"Just don't blame me if we get scribbled."

"What?"

"I think I used up all the luck I'm ever going to have against land mines. I've gone over three and I'm not dead yet. Four might be the unlucky number."

PART·TWO

Mozambique

Munashe's blissful time with Chenai in Chimanda did not last because instead of the scars of the war littered around the area bringing him relief and some measure of reconciliation with that brutal time as he had anticipated, he felt his suspicions crawl back and he began to be afraid that something might leap out of the nearest bush and pounce on him and Chenai saw it and asked him what the problem was.

"I think I need to go further," he replied, looking at the range of blue mountains across the border inside Mozambique.

"I don't understand."

"I think I was terribly mistaken," he said as if he was talking to himself. "There is no way I can reconcile myself with the ghosts of war without beginning in Mozambique."

➤ From *Echoing Silences* by Alexander Kanengoni

Accident Hill

Innocent in the kitchen on K's farm

FOUR MONTHS LATER, in early February, I flew from the States to Lusaka. K was there to meet me at the airport. As I pushed past the crush that had congregated around the customs officials, I could see him standing head and shoulders above everyone else, his breadth creating a vacuum of space around him. He looked even healthier and more powerful than I remembered, as if he had grown younger somehow since I had been here last.

"You look well," I said.

"I'm fasting."

"You're not eating?"

"No, I'm eating. Just no meat, tea, coffee, soft drinks, flour, sweets."

"Ah," I said. It showed in his face—he radiated vigor and a kind of purity, like an athletic monk.

"Thanks for meeting me."

"Hazeku ndaba." K seized my bags and strode ahead of me out into the humid swell of the African air, which I swallowed in hungry, happy gulps.

"Is it good to be home?" he asked.

"Always."

"Are you hungry?"

"Nope."

"I saw your mum and dad last week."

"Oh good. Are they okay?"

"Ja. Looking forward to seeing you when we get back from Moz." K swung my bags into the back of the truck and tied them down with rope.

I climbed into the car and K handed me a carton of cigarettes. "Gwai," he said.

"Oh man, I just quit again," I said, lighting one. I let the smoke curl around my tongue before exhaling. "Toasted tobacco, no additives," I said. "Yum. Tastes like childhood." We were racing past the cattle ranches that line the road from the airport and onto the Great East Road, which headed to Malawi on the one hand and into Lusaka on the other. YOUR FAMILY NEED YOU, a sign at the intersection reminded travelers, WEAR A SEAT BELT. USE A CONDOM.

Lusaka was at its most beautiful, extravagant with the end of the rainy season. The sky stretched above the city clear and fresh. Green pushed up on every available patch of earth. Even the shanties managed to look picturesque, hiding their poverty behind stubby hedges of bougainvillea and tins containing elephant-ear plants. A large white poster flapped at the pedestrian crossing: PREVENT CHOLERA, it instructed next to cartoon pictures of a pair of disembodied hands performing various ablutions.

We cleared the overpass that avoids a tangle of railway lines and the congestion of the bus and train stations and circled past the Family Planning Building and made our way down Cairo Road, where bright gardens and fountains have replaced dust bowls at traffic circles and where coffee shops and meat-pie take-out restaurants have replaced a ghost strip of broken windows and litter-strewn gutters.

And then we were peeling out of the city, past the Second-Class District with its open-air butcheries (goat and cow carcasses, swinging from trees, seething with flies), past MundaWanga Wildlife Sanctuary (a happily restored botanical garden, which, a few years before, had been an enclosure of abused, terrified, and starving wild animals), out toward the hills that surround the town of Kafue, and into the escarpment from which we could catch glimpses of the Sole Valley.

There is a section of the Pepani Escarpment nicknamed Kapiri Ngozi meaning, in Nyanja, "accident hill." Ngozi in Shona can also mean a "vengeful or unsatisfied ghost" and the road is correspondingly disturbed; spilled oil, torn tarmac, shredded guardrails, vandalized wrecks. Every week, at least one lorry is turned onto its back here, like a giant, marooned beetle. Fierce heat pumping up from the Sole Valley and the relentless grade of the road combine to overwhelm the brakes of the trucks that chew steadily up and down this spine of road— on their way through Zambia, into and out of Zimbabwe, the Congo, and Tanzania.

Sometimes, an accident on Kapiri Ngozi can hold up the flow of traffic on the escarpment for a week or more, and when this happens, entire, spontaneous villages erupt out of the face of the hill: green tarpaulins cast between sparse msasa trees, small cooking fires spire funnels of gray-blue smoke, and men stripped to the waist hunch in front of disabled vehicles. Prostitutes appear from Sole to administer to the stranded drivers. Women haul their baskets off the roofs of buses and set up stalls selling drinks and biscuits and roasted corn.

When we arrived at the escarpment we found a chaos of cars, vans, buses, and trucks. A lorry had lost control coming down Kapiri Ngozi, narrowly avoided tumbling over the edge into the deep valley below, and had jackknifed across the road. A curse of confusion had ensued. There were a mass of passengers and stranded travelers straggling from one vehicle to another or draped under shade on the side of the road. Fires had been kindled and the trader women were already arguing over the most favorable vending positions. A policeman was taking cover behind a plump woman trader, from where he occasionally bleated directions that went largely ignored.

K got out the cab. "Let me go and see what has happened."

He disappeared into the milling crowd. A small boy appeared and offered to sell me a jerry can of pilfered diesel.

"No thanks."

The boy poked his head in the window and his swiveling eyes took in the contents of the cab. "Money!" he demanded at last.

I shook my head.

"Give me!" he said.

"No."

"Why won't you give me? Give me!"

I closed my eyes, but the boy still breathed on me. "Hunger," he declared at last.

"Okay." I searched the cab and found a banana and some biscuits. "Here."

"You shouldn't do that," said K, appearing at my side. "You'll make a beggar out of him."

"For God's sake," I said, looking after the boy, who had sauntered to the next vehicle with his jerry can, "he's a child, not a Jack Russell."

K's shoulders sagged. "Myself, I always give to blind people. The Almighty is very specific about that. But if you try to help everyone . . . you can't help everyone."

A group of men who had scrambled up to the cliff above the road were now heaving boulders over the edge to create a bridge on the side of the road on which the lorry could be circumvented.

"How does it look up there?"

"Oh, we'll be here for hours," said K. "Half the drivers are fighting and the other half are inspired with liquid intelligence."

"With what?"

"They're drunk."

"Oh"—I stared out the windscreen without surprise—"well, that doesn't seem like such a bad idea, considering the alternative."

K laughed at me and, as usual, I was surprised by how sudden and generous his laugh was and by how this one gesture shaved the edge off the part of this man that I found most terrifying and unattractive. "I'd get out there and do something, but I'd only end up killing someone," K said. He sounded helplessly resigned, the way other people might say, "I'd help you do the dishes, but I always seem to break plates."

"Better not," I said.

"I punched a guy here last year."

"A South African," I said. "I heard."

"See?" said K. "Shit. My reputation! That's why I won't fight anymore." K sighed. "Wherever I go people have heard about me before I even arrive. And the thing is"—K spread out his hands—"I've never punched anyone who didn't deserve it. I've never gone looking for a fight in my life."

I leaned back on the front seat so that my feet could dangle out the window and catch the weak puff of warm wind that lifted off the valley floor and up the escarpment. I lit a cigarette and watched the smoke trickle off the tips of my fingers. "How many people do you reckon you've punched? I mean, put on the floor."

K looked down at me for a long time, considering. "I don't know," he said at last. Then he asked, "Not counting the war?"

"Not counting combat," I agreed.

"Maybe a couple of hundred."

"Two hundred!" I said, sitting up.

"Hey, I'm not proud of it," said K.

"And how many of those ended up in hospital?"

K shrugged. "Well, I put three in at once, does that count as three people or one?"

"Three people are three people."

"Then, let me see . . ." K stared at his hands for a moment. "A dozen, I reckon."

The heat outside sung its stinging tune. There were shouts from the men on the cliff. Rocks tumbled down onto the road and exploded in dust and shards of splintered granite. The trader women argued and shouted and chased children and flies from the food. The men who weren't fighting or rolling rocks off the cliff sat in whatever shade they could find and drank beer.

K stretched and said lazily, "My last week in the army, I was in an accident. I was in a truck that rolled. I was sitting in the back and I tried to jump clear but the damn thing came down on me. I did this"—K showed me his knee, which was snaked with a thick, brown scar. "It was a blerry mess. The army docs fixed it and sent me home on sick leave and I got so pie-eyed my first night home that I drove my own car off an embankment. They reckon it was thirty meters high, more. I should have been dead probably, but I just got my crutches out of the wreck and walked back to the bar and the bartender told me, 'You've had enough,' so I turned the place upside down. I told him, 'Who the fuck do you think you are? No one tells me when I've had enough.' I locked him in the storeroom and I started to drink the bar dry except the cops came and dragged me off to jail. It took six of them." K sighed unhappily. "That's where I was when I got my papers getting me out of the army. I was in chook with the biggest babalas of my life."

I closed my eyes. K started to tell me a story about a time, shortly after that, when he destroyed three taxi drivers and a cab in Bulawayo: "I was still on crutches too. Man! I remember ripping a door off the taxi and then my mind went. . . . You know, one moment I was aware of fighting . . . These ous had a crowbar, and they broke open the top of my head. Then my mind went blank. I wasn't unconscious, I just don't remember . . . I mean, my mind was blank from rage, not from getting knocked out. When I was aware of what was going on again, the taxi drivers had fucked off. But the taxi! The thing looked like it had been rolled. The roof was squashed in, the steering wheel twisted, the rims buckled, and I had the rearview mirror in my hand.

"I had to go to court three weeks later—assault and grievous blerry harm—and the taxi drivers were still a mess. One of them was in a wheelchair, one had to come to court on a stretcher, the other guy . . . fuck, I'd ripped his scalp off. It was frightening. I got fined two thousand bucks for that and a ten years' suspended sentence.

"The judge said, 'Animals like you should not be allowed to walk freely on the streets.'"

K's voice hummed on and on.

I slept.

When I woke up an hour later we hadn't moved, but K, who had been wearing a khaki-colored bush shirt and a pair of olive green corduroys from the early eighties, slightly flared at the ankle and beginning to strangle a little at the thigh, had stripped off and now had a towel wrapped around his waist. There had been a decided change in the mood of the previously cheerful travelers. At least one man, near the accident, had been punched and the men who were filling the ditch with rocks had gone on strike and had said that they refused to throw down another boulder unless we all agreed to pay them a few thousand kwacha for their efforts. With all the cars squashed up behind us and the disabled lorry in front of us, there was no immediate hope of our heading back to Lusaka or forward to K's farm.

I bought two ears of burned maize and a beer off one of the market women and found a place on the side of the road next to some truck driver. It was, I realized, the best place from which to observe the primping prostitutes who had recently toiled up from Sole, dressed to kill. Late afternoon sun throbbed onto the road. There was a smell of hot tarmac and fresh sweat and steady wood smoke and old burning rubber. Children curled up and slept on the bare ground, damp and oblivious and happily released, for the moment, from the tedium of waiting.

IT WAS EVENING by the time we reached the farm, too dark to walk to the river or see the bananas. The sudden evening had already stolen light off the river and a gibbous moon crept up behind the acacia trees to the east. K lit a lantern and showed me the way to the shower—a small ablution block set downwind from the bedroom and kitchen. "Here," he said, "I'll get you a cold beer. Anything else?"

"No. Thanks."

The hot water for the shower was heated by an old-style Rhodesian boiler (a drum of water set over a fire in a structure like a pizza oven). The room, freshly tiled, was meticulously clean and furnished with clean towels. As I was showering, K shouted, "I left a beer on the step for you."

We set up in the kitchen, me on a wooden crate wrapped in a chitenge and K at the counter chopping vegetables for a casserole. Sheba and Mischief slept at my feet. Dispatch shadowed K, sitting behind his master's legs and keeping one slit eye on me all the time. I put a tape recorder on the table.

"What's that?"

"Ignore it," I said.

Then neither of us said anything for a long time. The dogs dozed and scratched on the floor, the cicadas buzzed from the winter thorn trees, the odd mosquito droned. From up at the workshop, the generator hummed and sawed, the lights dimming and soaring in response. I sipped my beer and looked out at the star-spotted sky. K crushed garlic.

At last K said, "Okay, what do you want to know?"

I tried to think of something that would be easy for K to talk about, something uncontroversial. "What about school?" I asked. "Why don't you tell me about school?"

"Okay," said K. "From scratch?"

"Sure."

"I went to kindergarten in Zambia, in Matabuka," said K, "but I told you about that already, didn't I?"

I nodded.

"Well, then when I was eight, my fossils sent me to Zim—Rhodesia in those days—Mweni Junior in Bulawayo." K rummaged through a cardboard box that was on the steps outside the kitchen. "Don't ask me why they did it," he said, coming back with three tomatoes. "Because the school was full of Jews, and from day one they beat the crap out of me, those little bastards. They picked on the kids who weren't Jewish," K. said. "And that was me and about five other kids."

"Oh?"

K put down the knife with which he had been cubing sweet potatoes and glanced at the tape recorder. "I'm not against Jews, you know. I didn't have a quarrel with them—*they* picked on me. What was I supposed to do? Stand there and take it?"

I said nothing.

So K insisted, "What would you have done?"

"I don't know."

"Those little Jews *taught* me to hate Jews. I didn't hate Jews before I got there. I didn't even know what a Jew was."

"Do you still hate Jews now?"

"No, man, I don't hate anyone. I love all people the same. I don't care if you're a Yank, a Pom, a Chink, a fucking purple alien, a goffle." K wagged the pointy edge of the knife at me, then suddenly threw back his head and laughed. When he looked at me again, I saw that there were tears on his cheeks. "Oh ja!" he said. "A hobo of people have accused me of being a goffle. Ha!" K laughed, "Ha! Because in the sun I go almost black, hey? Have you seen? So people used to call me Goffle in the war. That was one of my nicknames." He slid potatoes and carrots into a pot and then he sighed and shook his head. His lips puckered and folded down at the edges.

I asked, "So why do you think your parents sent you to a Jewish school?"

K took such a long time to answer that I almost repeated the question. Then he said abruptly, almost angrily, "I don't know. I don't think they knew it was mostly Jews. You know? They hardly came to the school. They just put me on the train in Vic Falls and, 'Bye, chap, see you in three months,' and off I went."

"Did you ask your folks to take you out?"

"Ja, every time I went home. But my old lady wouldn't listen. Anyway, I begged her—on my hands and knees—not to send me to Mweni Senior because that's where all the big brothers of all the little Jews were, and I knew they would make mincemeat out of me. So she sent me to Wilson High in Que

Que." K chopped at a heap of onions angrily and tears flooded down his checks. "And the bullying didn't end there. You know? Anyone who went to a boys' boarding school in those days will tell you, if they're being honest, it was savage. If you couldn't stick up for yourself, you'd end up being rammed by every prick in the school."

There was a long pause while K sniffed, and wiped his face with the back of his hand. Then he said, "When I was fourteen, I was held down by two guys from my class while this older boy raped me."

Another long pause. Dispatch sat down abruptly and whined.

"That was it," said K, turning around and thrusting his knife into an eggplant. "I am not saying that being raped damaged me for life or anything, and it didn't make me hate homos. I have nothing against moffs as long as they leave me alone. I don't think that guy was a moff in any case; I think he was just a bully. But that was it for me. I had had enough. So I was in the shower one day and the guy—the arsehole that raped me— came in and I stepped out of the shower and I punched him. One time. Flat. That's when I realized I knew how to hit. Not even to talk. One punch right there"—K pointed to the tip of his chin with the knife—"and then in the goolies on the way down, and then a kick to the head when they're on the floor. That's all it takes. That's when I started to get a reputation as someone who could fight. People three and four years older than me picked fights with me because of that reputation. Half the fights I got into weren't even my fault."

K cut some bread and fed slices of it to the dogs.

"After that . . . I don't know, there probably wasn't a week when I didn't get into a fight with some damn idiot. All the little squirts wanting to see if they could get the better of me and all the big monsters trying to see if they could squash me. I learned the hard way—smack them hard first. Soon as you see them coming. One, two, three. Then it's over. Pointless dragging the thing out. You know, all these ous dancing about, flapping their fists all over the show? What's the point?"

"Did you ever box?"

"Ja. But I was shit at it. I wanted to kill my opponent the first time he punched me and there's all these rules about you can't nail an ou in the goolies or paste them in the head and anyway, who wants to fight for sport? I spent enough time fighting for real, I didn't need to do it in my spare time too."

"Did you ever lose a fight?" I asked.

K held the bread knife in the palm of his hand, as if weighing it. "Not once I figured it out," he said at last. "No, not that I can remember."

THAT NIGHT, K slept on the veranda and I took his bed in the single room overlooking the river. He had set up the small fan (battery-run) exactly so that it would blow onto my face. Before I could climb into bed, K sprayed the room with a powerful insecticide. "You won't need a mosquito net," he informed me.

My eyes started smarting and my throat burned.

"It works, that stuff."

"Yes," I wheezed.

"Sleep well, then."

"Good night."

Then the generator was switched off and the night expanded with insect life, the muted sound of drums from the village across the Chabija, the calling of nightjars and a solitary scops owl, "Prrrp! Prrrp!" I sat up on the bed and stared through the grille of the window at the river. A solitary islander had set up house on the patch of island in front of K's house. He was crouched over a fire that he had built to keep the hippos off his maize. I pulled my legs up, put my chin on my knees, and watched the barely moving shape of the man as he nudged his fire to keep it alive. Rain gusted lightly off the escarpment, breathed over the river, and misted the gauze on my window. The islander lowered some sort of shelter over himself and the fire—a large sheet of plastic, I thought—and the flames lit the edge of his face orange. When the hippos rose near the tip of the island three or four times and shouted at him, the islander banged on a large tin disk.

I lay down, but could not sleep. Sometime after midnight I heard fishermen in their dugout slapping the water with their paddles to chase fish into their nets. I went to the window and saw the long, low shapes of two canoes slipping through the velvety black water. The fishermen were both standing and, in unison, their paddles came down and the cracking sound that followed was not unlike gunshot. The islander called something to the fishermen, who shouted back. Shortly after that, the watchman stirred. I heard him up at the gate coughing thickly and then relieving himself noisily on the broad-leaved canna lilies. K got up, his bare feet scuffling on the bare veranda floor. He was talking steadily under his breath to the dogs. Finally, just before dawn, feeling stiff with sleeplessness, I got up to put the kettle on. K was already showered and dressed. He was sipping on a cup of hot water and honey.

"Sleep okay?" he asked.

I nodded. "Very comfortable, thank you."

I made tea and took the tray down to the river to watch the dawn. The islander had let his fire die to a smoky column and had curled up next to it to sleep. K's three dogs stationed themselves on the edge of the lawn and whinged. The watchman sounded the gong, a persistent clanging on a plow disk, to warn the laborers that they had half an hour before the day's work started. In a short time, a column of Africans filed up from the staff houses and into their places at the workshop, on the bananas, and at the nursery.

"I am going for a walk," K shouted to me from the kitchen. "Want to come?"

Cow Bones I

Bobo on K's farm with Dispatch

IN A NARROW SWATHE around the circumference of K's farm, the land had been scoured of all undergrowth and freshly mown, so that it resembled cultivated, protected parkland. The sun was just beginning to rise as we set out and the night's light rain had washed the air fresh and had released into it the scent of wild plants and the round, tinny smell of freshly hatched termites. An emerald spotted dove lamented, "My mother is dead. My father is dead. My sister is dead. And my heart goes dum-dum-dum-dum." The dogs forayed into the bush, occasionally yelping back to us their discoveries.

Then Dispatch came crashing back to K with something large and white in his mouth and dropped it at our feet.

"Oh look, a bone," I said. "Maybe a cow?"

K stood looking down at it for a long time, turning it over and over with his toe. Then he bent down and picked it up, weighing the thing in his hand. He ran his nose up the length of it, his eyes closed. Then he made a sound like a laugh, except it was too choking and bitter to be any sign of amusement, and he said, "Okay, I heard you."

"What?"

"I'm talking to the Almighty," K told me. There were tears in his eyes.

"Oh."

K said, "Go on, keep walking. Go back to the house. I'll catch up with you later." He held the bone in both hands now, his arms outstretched, as if he were offering it to the paper bark trees.

I turned back to the trail and kept going at a hurried walk. K did not follow me and when I looked back to see where he was, I saw that he had fallen to his knees in the cropped grass and his hands were held skyward, the bone aloft. Dispatch was by his side, anxious and trembling. Sheba was irreverently scratching fleas from her ear. I found my way back to the house alone.

K FOUND ME in the kitchen preparing a fresh pot of tea. "You okay?" he asked.

"Fine."

K shook his head. "I'm sorry."

"For what?"

"I made up my mind," said K, "last night. I wasn't going to talk to you anymore. I was going to tell you this morning, 'If you want to go to Mozambique, then go. Take the pickup, take a map. You can go and see for yourself. Me, there's nothing for me there.' But then . . . that bone this morning. The Almighty is talking to me." K sniffed and sighed. "I should tell you something."

I said, "Why don't we go and sit in the garden, then?" suddenly not wanting to be in the cramped confines of the kitchen with him.

K followed me. I poured myself tea and watched the river until K began to speak.

"About a week ago," said K softly and with great hesitation, "I had a dream that . . . I was digging up a grave. There were two bodies in the grave—two gondies, one man and one woman. And I was trying to get"—K's voice caught and it was a moment before he could continue—"the woman out of the grave. She was wrapped up in a chitenge, you know, like you were wearing last night, except she was wrapped from head to toe, like a mummy, so I couldn't see her face—except her arm was exposed, and there was no skin on her arm. Her bone was poking out and she had a big bone, like a cow's bone, like that bone we just saw . . . and I knew I had to cut through that bone to get her free. To get her out of the grave, I mean.

"So I was hacking at the bone with a panga and hacking and hacking, but I didn't have the strength to cut her free. I was too weak." K's voice tripped and when I looked over I saw that he was crying. "I was too weak," he repeated. Then K put his face in his hands and breathed deeply.

"What about the man in the grave?" I asked after a minute or so had passed.

K looked up and shook his head. "No, he was okay. It was okay for him to be there. Not the woman though, but I couldn't"—K gave a great yawn of anguish—"I couldn't . . .

free her. And then I woke up. I got out of bed and I fell on my knees."

I pictured K on the rough cement floor next to his bed in the little cell of a room, with the chirring insistence of Africa calling to him from outside. I pictured the great loneliness that stretched between him and the watchman who crouched by the gong at the top gate all night, and I pictured the watching islander tending his night's fire.

"I asked the Almighty, 'Father, what does this mean?'" K shuddered at the memory of it; tears rolled down his cheeks and collected above his lips. "And He told me," said K, "that I have to go back there and let her go."

"Let who go? Where?"

K shook his head and wiped his eyes with the back of his hands, but the tears sprung through his fingers and seeped down his neck. I looked away. At last K said, "I have so much inside me that I feel . . . If I could only get it out of me, then . . ." He wiped his eyes again, scraping his hand down from eyes to mouth. "Could you . . . ? I mean . . . if maybe . . . ?"

He looked at me with a mixture of anguish and hope and with such desperation that I folded my hands in my lap and looked at my feet.

K said, "That's okay. There isn't anything . . ."

A bird flashed in the bush in front of the veranda—a bright burst of red, yellow, and blue—and scolded, "prrrp," followed by a sharp wing clap.

K was startled. "Oh look," he said, forcing a steady voice through his tears, "it's the Angola pitta. I have a pair nesting here." He smiled and cleared his throat. "They're quite rare, you know."

"No, I didn't know."

"Ja." He stood up. "Come, bring your tea, there's something I want to show you."

K led me into his bedroom. He searched under his bed and

reappeared with a dented black tin trunk—the kind we used to take to boarding school as kids—with his name stenciled on the lid in white paint. K heaved the trunk onto his bed and opened it. It was full to bursting with papers, documents, and photographs.

"This is it," he said. "You want to know about me? Well, here it is. My whole life. Or what was left of it after the ex took everything." He picked up a couple of photographs that had been lying on the top of everything else. "Here," he said, handing me the photograph, "that was the ex."

A tiny, very pale redheaded woman with stunningly blue eyes stared out of the shiny paper. She was beautiful in a ghostly, luminous way, like the pale flame that comes from lighting dry mopane.

Then K shook himself and grew businesslike. "Okay, let's see," he said, turning his attention back to the trunk. "Oh look," he said, handing me a black-and-white photograph. "My fossils on their wedding day."

I took the picture and held it up to the light at the window. It showed a man and a woman of average height and indeterminate age (thirties or forties, their stern pose and their conventional 1940s clothes made it hard to tell) on the steps of a church. K's father—of whom K appeared to be a giant version—looked like a man of passion trapped into a suit of careful clothes and tight leather shoes. He had a dark complexion, full lips, and black eyes that looked deep into the camera. He was handsome in a way that suggested he might, in another life, have been romantic and jaunty: a B-grade actor, a lounge singer, or an artist in a Mediterranean tourist town, instead of a tobacco farmer on a dry scrape of land in Northern Rhodesia.

K's mother was laughing, not at the camera, but at someone over the photographer's shoulder. She was being held up by K's father, who had his arm firmly around her ribs as if catching her fall. She was mildly pretty, in a comfortable, unobtrusive way, but there was no bone structure for her face to hold on to and hers were the kind of looks that would dissolve with child-bearing and middle age. Her stomach bulged—because of her polio, K had told me—weakly.

"You look like your dad," I observed.

"Turkish," said K quickly.

"Turkish?"

"Originally his people came from the border of Turkey and Bulgaria."

"Ah."

"Me, I'm related to Genghis Khan," said K.

"I see."

"My dad was born in India," said K. "His great-grandfather went out there as an engineer."

"Oh," I said, "so he was part Indian?"

K looked shocked. "No," he said. "No wagon burners in the bloodline. They got their wives from Europe."

"Like racehorses," I said.

"Look." K handed me his father's papers, from which I could read that the man was born in Calcutta in 1915. In 1938, he enlisted with the Indian army. He fought in Egypt from September 1940 until June 1942, when he was taken prisoner at the fall of Tobruk and held as a prisoner of war in an Italian prison camp from June 1942 until May 1945. At the end of the war he was demobbed from the Indian army and went to South Africa.

His "Final Assessment of Conduct and Character on Leaving the Colours" read like a school report, rather than the assessment of a grown man: "Exemplary," someone has penned in neat ink next to the printed category "Military Conduct" and below that, "This man was a prisoner of war for over three years. A reliable, intelligent, hardworking man. Always cheerful. Fit for a responsible job. He should do well."

K held the papers on his lap. "I didn't know any of this until after the old boy died. He never talked about India, or the war, or the prisoner camp. To tell you the truth, he didn't talk about anything. I mean he literally did not open his mouth. He was a good father, though. Don't get me wrong. He put a roof over our heads, he fed us three square meals a day, he sent us to school, and he beat us regularly for the shit we did. You can't ask for more than that."

K showed me photos of himself as a kid—there weren't many and they were mostly blurry, as if taken in an impatient hurry. Then there were suddenly pictures of K in army uniform. In less than a dozen photos, the child had become a soldier. In one photo, K was building a long drop in the bush with his fellow troopies, laughing in triumph at the jute-covered hole in the ground. K, in full camouflage with his arm slung over his grand-mother's shoulders. Another picture showed him at night, in full uniform, with belt and shiny boots, beret and dark glasses. From the date on the back of the picture I calculated that K could not have been much older than nineteen at the time the photograph was taken, but he looked terrifyingly unboyish.

"What's this?" I asked, showing him the photograph.

"Oh, that was at my sister's wedding. I had to wear dark glasses because a bazooka blew up in my face in Moz, and my eyes were . . . shit, that hurts! To have a gun blow up in your face? Ooha blicksem! My eyes were swollen out to here"—K held curled hands out in front of his face—"and crawling with flies. I'd only been out of barracks a month or six weeks."

"Did they let you out until you were better?"

K looked surprised. "I couldn't see properly," he said, "but I could still see. No, they sent me back in. Two days off for the wedding, that was it. Then straight back into the shateen."

Then K showed me a picture of his father as an old man. It showed a fragile-looking man, bent in the spine and staring at the camera from beneath suspicious, nervous brows.

"That was Dad when he was an old toppie. He was never

the same after Mom died. He left the farm in Zambia, moved to Rhodesia, and lived in a little flat in Bulawayo. He was a mess, you know. A complete shell. He was older than her—I think fifteen years or so. I don't think he ever expected to outlive her, and he couldn't cope with being alone. One weekend when I was on R and R from the army he phoned me up and asked me if I'd help him move in with this woman—this nice old lady he had met at church. So I spent the whole weekend moving my old man's shit into this woman's flat.

"Three months later he phones me up and says, 'Son, help me move out of here.'

"I said, 'Dad, what's wrong? Don't you like her?'

"'No, it's not that. But she doesn't like to have sex.'

"Sheesh! Sixty years old and he's still worried about not getting his oats, hey. That's about as close as he ever got to telling me anything about anything." K stared out at the river, then said, "So he was a horny old bugger. I know that much. But nothing else. I don't know what else he had bottled up inside him. Maybe nothing. Maybe all kinds of bullshit. Who knows? He didn't laugh, he didn't talk, he didn't hardly drink, he never looked at another woman while he was with Mom. He smoked four cigarettes a day. Every day was the same for him. He worked his tail off, he never made money. But when he died, he didn't owe anyone anything and he had a roof over his head, and he had his pride. That's not a bad achievement, hey? I mean just to come onto the earth and leave it, having done the best you could with what you had."

"How did he die?"

"He keeled over of heart failure, six months before Luke . . . before my son . . . died. He was sitting in the backseat of my sister's car. She was taking him on holiday to Durban-by-the-Sea. He hadn't been on holiday for . . . shit . . . all his life.

"Then they get to the border and she says, 'Okay, Dad. We need to get out and do customs and immigration,' and the old man doesn't budge. So she says, 'Hey, Dad, we're here,' and she gives his shoulder a shake, you know, and he still doesn't budge. So that's when she twigs that he's snuffed it.

"So she phones me in a murra of a panic. 'Dad's died. What do I do?'

"I tell her, 'Keep your hair on, sis, just bring him back to Bullies.'

"So she drives him all the way back to Bulawayo and I meet her there and by now he's been dead hours and hours. I had to break both his arms to get him in a coffin. My sister was having a hernia, but what could I do?

"I told her, 'He's dead, man. He can't feel it.' I told him, 'Sorry, Dad,' but he would have understood. He would have done the same thing if he was in my position. He was practical that way, you know. A very practical man."

K handed me another photograph. "And that was Luke."

This picture showed a dark-skinned child with white, peg-shaped baby teeth and blond, almost white, hair. His eyes are nearly closed with laughing and his head is thrown back. His bare stomach is muscular and his stocky legs look powerful already. He is dressed in shorts; no shirt, no shoes, no hat.

"My son," K continued. He swallowed. "Five years old."

I looked at K.

K said, "We were at a braai—me and the ex and Luke and"—K breathed out—"the little chap came and found me at lunch and he told me, 'Dad, I have a headache.'" K's voice faltered. "My boy didn't whinge for nothing—he wasn't that type of kid, you know. He was a tough little guy. And independent. One minute he'd be in the garden playing and the next minute gone. I'd go looking for him and there he was running down the road, barefoot, no shirt, off to go and visit his mates. . . . He had so many friends. He didn't care—young, old, honky, gondie. Everyone in the whole town loved that child. So, anyway, I put him on a towel in the shade and I gave him some cold water. By three that afternoon he was in a coma." K took a shuddering breath. "Dead in a week. Meningitis."

"Oh God, I'm so sorry."

K said, "No. It was . . . That was when the Almighty finally got my attention. That's why I don't ignore Him now. Even though . . . sometimes it's tempting, of course.

"When Luke . . . when he . . . when he passed, that's when I stopped dopping. I promised God that if He'd give me another chance at a child, I'd bring that child up . . . I wouldn't drink, I wouldn't fight." K's voice broke and tears shone on his cheeks. "Oh shit . . . oh shit. He was a beautiful boy. You can see for yourself, can't you? He was an angel child. But . . . He was perfect. I wasn't good enough for him." K shook his head. "If I get another chance . . . If God gives me another chance—if He sees it within His gift to give me another child—I won't mess it up. I won't fuck up again. I'll bring the child up for His glory." The torment in K's voice, the suffering that he exuded, expanded into every corner of the little room, pushing out air and breath. "But that was it. Luke was the only one. We couldn't have more kids. It was as if . . . All those people I destroyed, all those lives . . . The Almighty was showing me what it was like to lose a child." Now K was crying so hard that his voice could hardly tear through his throat.

The little cement cell seemed to close in on us. I put my hand lightly on K's arm and murmured something and to my surprise I suddenly had the man hanging from my shoulder, his face buried on my neck, his mouth open against my throat in anguish. I was almost pushed off my feet. "Here, sit," I said. "You must sit." I steered K to the bed and his legs folded under him. I knelt on the floor and put my hands on his knees. "What can I do? Jesus, I'm sorry. I had no idea. . . ."

K shook his head. "If you think about it, it makes sense,

doesn't it? What else could He do? How could He have done anything else with me?"

I said, "I don't think children die to punish their parents."

Then suddenly K was shouting at me through his tears, "Okay, then you explain it! You tell me why I'm here alone! You tell me why He punishes me every fucking day. Every day I wake up and I think of that child. Not . . . a . . . fucking . . . day . . . Oh . . . oh . . . oh . . ."

Now I was crying too. "I know," I said.

"No!" K sobbed. "You don't know. How can you know? Have you lost a child?"

I shook my head. K blurred in my tears, as if he had been washed into something impermanent and shimmering on the bed.

"Then you don't know. You have no idea."

"No."

Dispatch had come to the door, which was as far as he dared, and was lying with his head on his paws, ears flat. Sheba and Mischief were confused, milling in front of the window. Sheba whined.

"It's all right, guys," said K through his tears, getting up and going to the window. "Hey now, it's all right," he told the dogs softly. He came back to the bed and put a hand under my chin, so that I was forced to look up at him. His face and neck and shirt were soaked with tears. His mouth was glistening with the salty, thick saliva that comes with crying.

"It's okay," I said.

K wiped his face. "Ja."

I felt as if I had had the air knocked out of me.

K ran a thumb under my eyes. "You've had your sorrow too."

"Everyone has," I said. "We all do."

"Ja."

"Here," K said. He offered me the end of his shirt. "Wipe your face."

"I'll get some bog roll."

"No," said K, dabbing at my eyes before I could get to my feet. "It's soaked anyway." For a long time I felt wiped with the scent of K, with his tears and sweat—a salty, earthy mix not unlike the smell of fresh blood.

Plagues

Transport—Zambia

AFTER LUNCH, we packed K's pickup with fishing rods, drinking water, sleeping bags, mosquito nets, a tent, more than a hundred liters of fuel (there was a politically inspired fuel shortage in Zimbabwe), and food. "My body is a temple for the Almighty," K explained, loading peanuts and green peppers into a tin trunk that served as our larder.

"And my body is not," I said, adding beer and potato chips to the cache.

We planned to leave the next morning; driving from K's farm in Zambia, through Zimbabwe and from there into Mozambique, retracing the geographical path of much of K's history and with the vague idea that we would find our way back to the battlefields of more than twenty years ago.

In the evening, we walked around the bananas and down to the water pump below an orange orchard on the Chabija. K had built a store on the farm with a small veranda and pretty gardens, overlooking the river. Behind that, upon an open rise where there was an almost constant breeze off the river, there was an impressive, neat row of staff houses. There was no garbage lying about, and the yards in front of the staff houses were swept and clean. It was as if the Africa I knew, with its assault of smells and its flotsam of debris and its inevitable chickens and goats and carelessly strewn life, had been pressed and contained beyond the borders of the electric fence. This farm was a model of industry and discipline.

K told me, "When I first started the farm, there were some bad guys on the place—they were just here to loaf and steal. The worst offender was this guy called John Mapariwa. He was down at the river as the pump guard. I knew he had been stealing, so I fined him. He organized a strike. . . . You know, the usual story. There's always one bad lot that ruins it for everyone. Anyway, I sorted everything out with the labor.

"I said, 'Fine. If you want to strike, sit right where you are and you're gone—consider yourselves fired. If you want to work, then start working.'

"And the workers gradually got up—most of them—and came over to my side. But Mapariwa sat out—so he was fired. And he was bitter about it too. The night the strike was settled I went into my bog and there was a burrowing adder on the shelf above the sink. Now what the hell is a burrowing adder doing in my bathroom? On a shelf? They burrow—they don't live in houses, on shelves. I knew Mapariwa had put it in there. Or at least I suspected Mapariwa had put it there. My first instinct was to go out to his village, find him, rip his head off, and shove it down his neck, but instead I got down on my knees and I asked the Holy Father what must I do.

"He told me. 'Read Micah, Chapter two, verses two and three.'"

Then K cleared his throat and recited: "'They covet fields, and seize them; houses, and take them away; they oppress householder and house, people and their inheritance. Therefore, thus says the Lord: Now I am devising against this family an evil from which you cannot remove your necks.'

"See?" said K to me.

I nodded.

"So, I took the Bible to Michael—my foreman—and I put my finger on this scripture and I said, 'An evil will fall upon John Mapariwa. I don't know what, but something bad is going to happen to him.'"

K looked at me. "And guess what happened?"

My mind swam with all the available evils. I shook my head.

"Two weeks later he was bitten by a black mamba. They brought him to the house—his relatives—in the middle of the night in a wheelbarrow. I was here sleeping and I heard the dogs going benzi, and the watchman beating the gong and I could hear women—you know the sound—ululating. That's when you know the shit has hit the fan in some major way—either someone was dead or dying.

"I went up to the workshop to investigate and there's Mapariwa in the wheelbarrow, barely alive. I put him in the back of pickup and told Michael to run and switch on the generator, so I could have some light and see what was going on. So the lights come on and I see Mapariwa. Shit, he was in rough shape. I knew then that he was going to snuff it, so I put a blanket over him and as I was pulling it up we looked into each other's eyes and he knew. He knew that I knew. We both knew." K shuddered. "To look in the face of the power of the Almighty like that, it was chilling.

"I told him, '*I* forgive you. But you'd better make it right with Mwari pretty fucking fast, because you're on your way to the big, fat, fucking oven downstairs if you don't.'

"And his lips start to move, but there's no sound. You know? Just that noise—have you ever heard it? When someone's about to croak? It's like their lungs rattle.

"So I tell him, 'Speak up, my boy, the Almighty needs to hear you.'

"Then he makes this sighing sound and snuffs it."

THE NEXT MORNING, while K went to his office to make sure that his foremen knew what work needed to be done on the farm in his absence, I went from the kitchen, to the workshop, and on to the banana fields, asking the people who work for him what they thought of him, of the farm, of their lives. Of course I have no way of knowing what they really thought of K, or of me. Grinning politely they told me that yes, working for Bwana K was very good. Better than before when there was no job. No food. No school. So now things are okay. They are much better, in fact. Thank you for asking. And they obediently went back to the task at hand. For all they knew, I was spying on K's behalf. For all they knew, I was in line to be the new madam of the farm.

Michael, the foreman, was more talkative. We sat in the shade of the workshop sharing a tray of tea and he told me about his previous work as a welder for an Indian mechanic in Lusaka.

"Those Indians are even worse," Michael told me, echoing the common prejudice that many black Zambians have against Asians, "greedy and cheating. Bad man."

"What about here?"

Michael smiled. "This Bwana, he's tough. He's tough, but very squarc." He shook his head. "He made a good house for the workers even while he was sleeping in a tent. Himself, he still sleeps like a black man, in a black man's house. And I think he understands Mwari. Maybe they have a way of talking together." Michael told me about the incident with the burrowing adder and the black mamba. "It's hard," he said, "to find such a man who understands God in this way. I hope I will be here until I die."

When I told K what Michael had said, K said, "Ja, he's a good gondie. I really love that man. He's honest, he's godly, he's really one of the best managers I've ever had. And let me tell you something about Michael. When I found him, he didn't know much about farming. But he was willing to learn. I taught him everything and he caught on quickly and he showed that he has a head for responsibility.

"Now what usually happens around here is that you find a decent gondie, you train them, and then the poor bastard gets Henry the Fourth and dies. Now how do you explain this? Michael can't get a stiffy. I have the only gondie in Zambia who can't screw himself to death. Do you think that's a coincidence? And he's so bloody good. He's sent by God, and he has been protected by God."

I said, "Poor Michael. I am sure he'd rather not be impotent."

"Yes, but if he could catch a woody, he'd be dead by now. It's his protection from God. What's the average life expectancy in Zambia? Thirty-three, thirty-four, if you're lucky. These poor bastards are dying like chickens and what can you do? I give them cartons of condoms and I'm in the compounds every month with a broomstick showing them how to wear them, how to reuse them, but if screwing was your only pleasure in life, would you use a condom? Of course not.

"To say nothing of all the other shit that happens. They're always poking each other's wives and their own nieces and daughters and sister-in-laws. And then they want kids, of course. The more the merrier. Man!" K threw up his hands. "It's a fucking plague and now I probably have it. Do you know how many bleeding munts I've touched, carried, treated? Dozens. Dozens and dozens. But what can you do? Do you think about AIDS when someone can't breathe and you have to give them the kiss of life? Do you?"

I didn't say anything.

"Of course you don't," said K, assuming that I was a better person than I probably am. "If that is the way that God chooses for me to die, then it is His will and what can you do?"

"Wear gloves?" I suggested weakly.

K snorted. "I probably should carry a first-aid kit with me wherever I go with a full-body condom in it so I could hop into the thing whenever a gondie decides to get run over, or fall out of a tree or get eaten by a croc. But I don't. And a little pair of gloves aren't going to cover a damn thing when the blood is really gushing out. Now, is it?"

Brothers in Arms

Soldiers line up for food

BY THE TIME WE LEFT the farm, the sun had taken its place in the sky, spreading across the divide of east and west, elbowing out sky and color and perspective, and sending a flattening assault of rays to the earth. The greater part of Africa—the vast, uncurling spill of cities and roads, and jungles and savannahs—lay behind us. We were heading steadily toward the Indian Ocean, toward the thick slice of land that curled around Zimbabwe's eastern shoulder, nudged Zambia, and almost swallowed Malawi off the map altogether. Scatter-shot in our path were soldiers from K's war. Hundreds of them probably, most of them silent about the years that were stolen from them and the years that they had stolen from others.

It's not hard to find an old soldier in Africa. In fact, there are probably parts of Africa where almost anyone over the age of ten is an old soldier and has held an AK-47 in his hands and let its fire chatter into human flesh. (Christmas-cracker guns is how they seem, cheap and deadly and associated with mass production in China.) And then there are parts of Africa where ammunition and guns aren't available and citizens—children among them—take up arms against one another with whatever instruments they can find: machetes, hoes, knives, their bare hands.

What is harder to find are old soldiers who will *talk* about their war with strangers. And why should they talk? Those of us who have escaped the horror of being turned—by whatever euphemisms there are for the calculated process of dehumanization—from people into machines that issue, and might reasonably expect to receive, a sentence of death are ill equipped to judge (let alone understand) anyone who has been a soldier. Our minds are still innocent of the stain of sanctioned murder.

I can recognize a certain breed of ex-soldier, not only for what they look like, but also for how their lives have unraveled. There are the tattoos, the shaggy beards (something about all the years of military seems to instill the need for copious, perhaps disguising, facial hair), the cigarettes, the drinking, the bluster. If you sleep in the same house or camp with them, you will hear their spooks. They shout their ghosts away all night.

There are the multi-marriages (of the six soldiers I met and talked to in any kind of depth while traveling with K, three were divorced, one had been widowed when her husband committed suicide, one had never married but tore haphazardly through his relationships with women). There is the history of violence: the brawls, the destroyed bars, the nights in jail. And then, when everything else has peeled away from them, there is God.

The first ex-soldier whom I met on my journey with K had been a soldier for almost all his life. Riley had started out as border patrol for the Rhodesian army in 1962, and had stayed on to fight until shortly before that country's independence. When he ran out of war in Rhodesia, Riley headed for South Africa. Riley's wife is also an ex-soldier. She joined up in the 1970s and met Riley in training camp soon after. Her first husband (who had been a soldier too) had shot himself.

In 1992, when South Africa was clearly on its way to democratic rule and wars in Africa had changed their tone (they had turned in on themselves—tribal, hand-to-hand, and indistinct and no longer the black-and-white wars of the liberation days), Riley and his wife came to Zambia looking for work. For a while, they camped on K's farm and acted as his farm managers.

One night, when K was away, armed thieves came to the farm. Riley was shot in the hand before he could return fire. He showed me his hand. "Almost thirty years as a soldier and I don't get hit," he told me, "and then I get nailed in Sole by a gondie with a sawn-off shotgun!" When Riley laughed, as he did then, it was an alarming event. His laugh caught, like a two-stroke engine on an old motorbike, and turned into its own choking throb until the man had turned a pale, airless green. He broke the filter off a Madison—Zimbabwe's strongest cigarette—and lit it, which took some doing because his hand shook so violently that the match almost flitted itself out.

"That was enough for me," said Riley's wife, shuddering. "Being out there in the bush with those . . . bloody bandits. I mean it's not like it used to be, you know. It was safer during the bloody war than it is now.

"I told Riley, 'No, man. I'm not staying here to get chayaed by some gondie with half a gun. Not after everything . . .'

"I don't know how K stays down there alone like he does."

Then we all had to be quiet while Riley was shaken by another fit of coughing. He took a deep drag off the shortened cigarette, and that subdued his cough for a moment.

I said, "Did you ever catch the guy that shot you?"

Riley's eyes slid across to K and there was a significant silence.

At last K said, "Riley is a highly trained soldier."

"Meaning?"

"Meaning, 'Rest in peace, gondie,'" said K.

"And the police?"

"Were very grateful," said K. "They wrote that the gondie died of natural causes."

Which sent Riley into another spasm of laughter-turned-coughing. Then he leaned over and said to me, "What you need to understand, Bobo, is that this isn't how it used to be. There aren't rules of engagement anymore. The way it used to be, the enemy was there"—Riley moved a box of Madison cigarettes across the table to represent the enemy—"and he was in his uniform. You were over here"—Riley placed a fork opposite the cigarettes—"and you were in your uniform. Then you opened fire and whoever got scribbled lost and whoever didn't get scribbled won."

He smashed his fist down on the fork, which sailed in a high, graceful cartwheel off the end of the table, and then he sat back and pulled his lips down. "Now it's just dog-eat-dog. Gondie-scribble-gondie. No one gives a shit. It's not about color. People think it's about color. It's not about color. If it was about color, it would be easy to understand."

"No," agreed Riley's wife, wagging her finger at me, "not about color."

Riley said, "You want to know what it's about? It's about pure animal survival. And these lazy bastards want something for nothing. Why go out and get a job when you can wave a shotgun in someone's face and get money for nothing?"

"Life's expendable," said K. "It doesn't matter to these guys if they get plugged because they're going to starve to death anyway. It's what . . . ? What do you say when there are no rules of engagement anymore?"

"Anarchy," replied Riley. "Pure and simple anarchy."

"Ja," said Riley's wife, regret underpinning her voice, "the war was the easy part. Not this . . ." and she gestured toward the veranda of the hotel on which we were having lunch (the empty tables, the cluster of noisily drunk clients at the bar, the pale glare of rain-washed sun).

"And now?" I asked. "What do you do now?"

"Now we're fishing up here," said Riley breathlessly, waving at the expanse of Lake Kariwa. "Civvy street," he said, as if the word could be picked off his tongue with the debris of loose tobacco that had scattered there from the end of his butchered cigarette.

I asked if he regretted the war and Riley blinked at me, as if I had said something blasphemous. "Regret?" he asked rhetorically. "No. No. Those were the best years of my life. Maybe I could have skipped South Africa. That was bullshit. They treated us like shit. But Rhodesia"—Riley cocked his head in the way that people do when the ability to define a fine wine has eluded them—"Rhodesia . . . That was *living*."

"You don't think it . . ." I searched for a word that could put what I was trying to say delicately. ". . . it affected you? All those years of fighting?"

"War doesn't have to mess you up"—Riley eyed me suspiciously—"if that's what you're trying to say. Is that what you're trying to say?"

It was, but I shook my head.

Riley bit the head off another Madison and I thought of the Zimbabwean advertisement, *Man, make yours Madison*. "It didn't mess me up. I've been a soldier most of my life and it didn't mess me up." He coughed his metallic-coffin laugh again. "We had information on where the gooks were. We were dropped out of airplanes, did the job, and then they pulled us out. When it got stressful . . . well, yes: it got stressful when there were three or four contacts a day. That's how it was. Dropped you in, take you back to base to reissue and give you a brief, and then you're back in the plane. It was okay. It was a job. It was just a job. Better than sitting behind a desk. Now *that* would have messed me up. Sitting behind a fucking desk with a tie around my neck"—Riley grasped his neck with his powerful hands and throttled himself—"*that* would have killed me."

IT WAS ONLY AFTER we had crossed the border from Zambia into Zimbabwe that K remembered that he still had his revolver with him. "Shit," he laughed, rooting around in his briefcase and emerging with the weapon, "the Almighty was looking after us, my girl. If those customs guys had found this thing"—he waved the revolver around carelessly and the car swerved, narrowly avoiding a stub-tailed chicken that had chosen that moment to scuttle across the road—"we'd both be melting to death in a gondie jail by now."

"How about we don't try and cross into Mozambique with it?" I suggested.

"I'll leave it with a friend," said K. "You talk to Dingus while I drop the gun."

That was the other peculiarity of the soldiers I met. None of them went by their given names. K is known variously as the Phantom Sergeant (he refused to stand for troop photographs during the war, and in commando pictures he shows as a white gap in the front row) or Savage or Goffle. The man whom I was about to meet was known, not as Peter, but Dingus after his habit of asking for "that dingus" or "this dingus," or for referring to a woman as "quite a dingus." Dingus is Afrikaans for "thing."

Dingus turned out to be an incredibly soft-spoken man. He almost whispered in answer to my questions. His wife was a vivacious, blonde Englishwoman. Both smoked cigarettes as an apparent substitute for breathing. Dingus's wife brought out a pot of tea and we sat around a rickety veranda table; its Formica top had curled up at the lip, showing rotting plywood underneath. Dingus and his wife, in common with many Zimbabweans, were leaving Zimbabwe.

"Nothing left here now," said Dingus, shrugging. "Look, we can stay and starve and wait for the end, or we can leave while we still can."

Packing cases and boxes waited in stacked, sagging towers.

"Where are you going?"

"North," said Dingus. He lit a cigarette with the end of one he was just finishing. "I got a job as a boat mechanic on Lake Tanganyika."

"God help us," said his wife with feeling.

Dingus, like K, had found God. I asked him what prompted his conversion and he told me that after the war he had been such a violent man—so angry all the time—that he had gone through two marriages (he said this the way a rally driver might talk about needing to change shredded tires in the middle of a grueling race). "During the war it didn't matter. The aggression was—well, you needed it. It was a way to survive. It was afterward. . . . When my second wife left me, that was when I woke up." He, like K, had joined the army straight out of school. "I could hardly read," he said, "but I knew how to shoot. I could fight."

Looking at him, it was hard to believe that he was any kind of young man, or soldier. His eyes washed pale and blue into the back of a yielding face. His lips were indecisive and sad, looped down at the edges. He carried a soft paunch over which was stretched a holey, pale blue vest. He looked like a man who had surrendered. And, like so many Africans, he'd had his gut of tragedy. Four years before his daughter died of malaria. He talked softly—almost mouthing the words—about her death, his voice barely rising above the tenure of breath. There were no other children. His wife looked stunned and stiff while he talked and her eyes filled with tears.

Then he talked about the war, his regret that he had any part in what he now saw as mindless killing. And he talked about what was happening in Zimbabwe now—the way that land redistribution, from landed whites to landless blacks, had turned into a full-scale war of looting, thievery, and political oppression.

"It's just wrong," Dingus told me in a disappearing voice, "criminal. That man"—he meant Mugabe—"should be stopped before he destroys this entire country."

Only when Dingus talked about God did his voice sound as if it were on firm footing, gripping on something actual and strong and real. But he whispered about his life before God and the death of his daughter, as if, by whispering, he could undo his own history.

When K returned from stashing the gun and we took our leave in the late afternoon, Dingus leaned over the edge of his veranda to see us off. The rusted rails of the veranda looked too fragile against the press of his belly and the ache of his past. He waved good-bye, saying to K, "Don't let the ghosts in Moz bite you, Goffle!" and at that moment, the sun glittered off our windscreen and blotted his face into an obliterating white and he flinched back, his hand to his cheek.

When I looked over at K, he had tears in his eyes.

As we drove away, K said, "Dingus and I are closer than this"—K crossed his fingers. "Look at our lives? The army, then broken marriages, then . . . The drinking, the violence, all that is there too. Then, you know, we both realized at some point that the way we were going was killing us, killing the people around us. We were destroying so much. You know after I lost Luke, that's when I woke up and started to listen to the Almighty. Dingus had to lose a wife before he woke up." K shook his head. "He's a lovely man, that. A lovely, lovely man.

I'll miss him when he heads up north. He's the only man . . . he's probably the only person in the world who knows why I am the way I am. He's maybe the only human being who knows everything I've done—every good thing, every shit thing. And he still loves me." K sniffed. "Now that's really something, hey?"

Demons and Godsends

Road sign, Zimbabwe

K LOOKED AT ME SIDEWAYS. We were climbing out of the valley into which Lake Kariwa spills, gushing out of the gorges of the Pepani River and slamming to a standstill at the wall near a rock that the Tonga people call Kariwa—the trap. This escarpment was a road of memories for K. He moved here with his young wife a few years after the war and this was where his son was born, and died. He said, "I love this valley," and his jaw bulged in a way that I now recognized as a prelude to something that made my heart grab at the edges of my ribs.

"The ex was such a . . . She's tiny," he said, "but very strong. She works out in the garden all day, like she's . . . trying to run from something. Well, she is. She is trying to run from something." He paused and said, matter-of-factly, "She's possessed."

I realized then that we had slipped—as periodically happened—off the edge of normal conversation into K's mind, where he was at his most paranoid and angry.

"Possessed?"

"Ja. By demons. Ja." His lips slapped shut with finality. It was a long time before he said, "You know, she never got over Luke. She can't leave that poor boy to rest in peace. Luke's room, all his clothes, everything, even his ashes. They're all in his cupboard. Everything washed and folded and in his cupboard like he's going to come home after lunch for his afternoon rest. She's even left his toys where they were when he died. All his stuffed animals are on his bed. . . . It's all there. And she spends hours sitting on his bed, like she is waiting for him. To this day, she's there. Every day. She'll never leave Zimbabwe. She'll never leave that boy alone. If those 'landless peasants' come for the house, they'll have to kill her or let her live there with them because they won't get rid of her."

I said, "I don't think that's being possessed. That's grief."

K shook his head. "No. You don't understand. I actually saw the demons entering her. I woke up one night and I watched the demons fighting for her soul. If I hadn't woken up . . . I pulled the sheets up around her and I told them to fuck off and they went back out the window. The demons—well, there was one in particular, like a cat's head floating there, black and with bright green eyes, that was trying to get into her. But I chased it out. I used the power of the Almighty to chase it out. But the ex has never believed, really. She used to say that she did, but she doesn't. And since then, oh ja . . . she's evil. She opened herself up as a house of Evil and they came. She's possessed."

I don't underestimate the power of ghosts and spirits and, at that moment, I could feel K's own demons. They were burning and noisy and hard-edged and they were churning about in the front of the car. The windows were open and the air was rushing around us, hot and black from the tarmac, but it couldn't sweep the demons out of the car.

"When we were going through all our shit"—by which I assumed K meant the affair that he said his ex-wife had had—"I knew she was possessed. What else would make a woman do what she did?"

I puffed hard on my cigarette and said nothing.

"About ten years ago, when we were still trying to work out our marriage, I prayed to the Almighty, what should I do? I read that the answer to my problem could only be resolved by prayer and fasting. For twenty-five days I prayed and fasted and then I waited for God to tell me what to do next. Nothing. I waited three days. On the third day, He told me to visit the ex. I was with Dingus at the time.

"I told him, 'Dingus, the Almighty has sent me to her.'

"I was—I was so sure that God was going to send the demons out of her. I could feel His power all around me. Dingus dipped his finger in cooking oil and he drew a cross on the windscreen, right there"—K pressed his finger against the windshield and drew a cross on the glass—"right there." K glanced over at me to make sure he had my attention, which he did. Every nerve was prickled. I felt as if I was sitting in a small chamber of ever advancing needles. "Dingus came with me. We drove to the ex's house and I got out of the pickup. The gate was locked. I called for her, I hooted. I shouted some more. I knew she was in there. I could just *feel* she was in the house. When she came out, she had a gun with her.

"I asked her, 'What's the gun for?'

"She said, 'Leave me alone.'

"I said, 'I need to talk to you.'

"We went back and forth for quite a while like this, hey. Eventually, she let me in. We went into the house. I told her to put the gun down. I mean, I am the one that taught her how to shoot the blerry thing and she can shoot straight, that woman. I fixed the trigger on the pistol to make it less stiff for her. That's when I did this." K lifted his left leg and showed me the holes in his calf and ankle, which I had correctly assumed were bullet wounds. "See? Bullet went in here"—K pressed his calf—"and out here. I always used to wonder what it would feel like to get shot, and then I shot myself by accident and found out. It hurts like sterek, man. Shit, it hurts.

"Anyway, I told the ex, 'The Almighty is my shield. Put the gun down.'

"She told me, 'Your God is your God, and I respect that. But I don't communicate with Him.'

"And I told her that she needed to get onto her knees and ask His forgiveness.

"She said, 'No.' Then she said, 'Leave me alone.'

"I said, 'Can I pray for you?'

"She said, 'I want you to leave now.'

"I put my finger on her cheek and she screamed at me, 'Don't touch me.'

"I thought, I honestly thought, that I'd feel something. That God would give me the power to heal her. What I felt was"—K flicked the top of my arm—"like that, a small electric shock. That was all. Nothing else."

By now we were beyond the road that snakes out of the Pepani Valley and that describes the long eastern border between Zambia and Zimbabwe which surfaces at Mkuti. Here, the Pepani Escarpment gathers to a long, undulating ridge as far as the eye can see; a quivering headdress of spring-red msasa leaves and lichen-covered branches. A gray cloud swung its belly over the brush at the summit and fat drops of rain burst on the windscreen and splattered into the car and dotted up and down my arms. I hung out of the car and let the rain fall on my face.

K said, "When I drove home, the cross that Dingus had made on the windscreen with cooking oil, it nearly drove me benzi, I tell you. I kept staring at it and I wanted to wipe it off the windscreen. It hadn't bothered me when I was driving out to the house, but coming back, it was making me crazy. What does that tell you?"

I brushed the rain off my forearm and pressed myself against the door. "Maybe the light hit it differently," I said. Since K kept his car, like everything else in his life, meticulously washed and clean, I was not surprised to hear that he found a smudge of oil on his windscreen annoying.

"No," said K, "it tells me that I had Satan within me. And when I got home to Dingus's house, he made some tea and I took the cup from him and I found my hand was shaking so much I couldn't get the cup to my lips." K took his hand off the steering wheel to demonstrate how much his hands had been shaking. His hand fluttered in my face, like a bird trapped indoors. "Just like that. And the next thing I knew I was on the ground and this . . . scream . . . It wasn't me. It wasn't my voice. It was something else. This powerful scream came out of my throat. A roar, I guess. It was like a lion and it felt like my neck was going to burst." Looking at K's neck now, I had the same concern. "And this great yell. And then I blacked out."

He gave me a long, significant look. He said, "That was the power of the Almighty. That was the Almighty fighting Evil."

Anyone who has, involuntarily or voluntarily, starved in the course of her life knows the light-headed, almost hallucinatory effect of an extensive fast. I said, very quietly, "You don't think you just needed a square meal in your tummy?"

"You think I'm benzi, don't you?"

"No," I said. And then, "Well, yes. A bit."

"Do you believe in love?"

"What?"

"Love," insisted K urgently. "Do you believe in it?"

"I don't understand."

"Can you see love?" K persisted but before I could reply K shook his head. "No," he said. "No, you can't." He let this sink in before saying, "The ex made me go to a shrink after that. She also thought I was benzi."

"Yes."

"The shrink told me God wasn't real. She told me that I couldn't see God or demons. That I was hallucinating or imagining stuff." K was sweating. Under the spice of his aftershave, he exuded wood smoke, the singe of charcoal-ironed clothes, and an aroma like a freshly turned field. "So I asked her, 'Do you believe in love?'

"She said, 'Yes.'

"So I said, 'But you can't see it, can you?'

"She said, 'No.'"

K started to laugh humorlessly. "It's the same with God. You can believe in Him without seeing Him. He's there! He's there!" He slammed his fist into the dashboard twice to emphasize his point.

I said, "Steady on. Remember what happened to the taxi."

K glanced at me and his look was so purple with fury that I choked back my words and lit another cigarette. Then I looked out of the window at the way the bush uncurled a more vivid shade of green as the black clouds rolled on. The tree trunks were like charcoal-blackened posts in the painted red soil. Suddenly, a man emerged out of the bush with an enamel basin full of wild wood mushrooms. He had a yellow plastic fertilizer bag over the top of his head against the spitting rain. He sprang forward at the sight of our lonely car, almost into the path of our tires, and I caught the edge of his high voice, "Boss! Mushroooooms! Boss! Madam!"

I said, "Oh look, someone selling mushrooms. Should we buy some?"

Barely pausing, K hauled the car around in the road, peeled out a U-turn on the wet tarmac, and bore down on the little mushroom man. As K climbed out of the car, the man pressed back in response. K has that effect on people—a sort of don't-even-think-about-*thinking*-about-messing-with-me look about his shoulders. But when K spoke, the neck-aching fury of late had left his voice. He sounded almost gentle and cheerful. He spoke Shona quickly, too fluently for me to follow entirely, but I understood enough to know that he asked about the man's business and asked how things were these days.

Yes, things were hard with this government, the man agreed.

K wanted to know, How was the man's family.

The man looked away. The smallest child had died. The mother of his children was in Malawi with her people. No, times were very hard.

And K tutted under his breath and asked the man whether he preferred Zimbabwean dollars or Zambian kwacha for his mushrooms. K pulled out a plastic bag in which we were carrying cash for our trip: a wad of Zambian kwacha, a stack of Zimbabwean dollars, and a pile of Mozambican meticals. K waved the alternatives at the man. The man responded, "Kwacha, boss. Please, boss. Zim dollar is buggered." So K gave him the money and he didn't haggle about the price of the mushrooms and then he put a hundred-dollar bill in the man's shirt pocket and said, "Bonsella."

K put the mushrooms into the tin trunk with the beer and chips and nuts and green peppers. "Tatenda, eh."

"Tatenda, boss."

As we were about to leave, the mushroom seller leaned into the car and pressed another bag of mushrooms onto K's lap. "For you, boss. God go with you."

I slumped back into my seat and closed my eyes.

I don't think we have all the words in a single vocabulary to explain what we are or why we are. I don't think we have the range of emotion to fully feel what someone else is feeling. I don't think any of us can sit in judgment of another human being. We're incomplete creatures, barely scraping by. Is it possible—from the perspective of this quickly spinning Earth and our speedy journey from crib to coffin—to know the difference between right, wrong, good, and evil? I don't know if it's even useful to try.

"God go with you!" the mushroom man had said, and I was grateful to him.

Because if anyone was going to be with us on this journey, it might as well be God. Especially if the alternatives were K's demons, those loud little creatures with their party hats and whistles and tap-dancing shoes that caught in the front of the pickup and sucked up all the air.

Cow Bones II

Kids

FOR THE NEXT TWO DAYS, we spun across Zimbabwe's stranded countryside, swallowing with lonely tires the almost empty road that branched up northeast from Harare to Mozambique. Political violence, a regional drought, and fuel shortages had washed up the citizens of this countryside into despondent-looking crowds that clustered near food-aid drops and under the shade of tavern verandas. The towns that we scudded through sound like words in a song: Mutoko, Murewa, and Nyamapanda. It was a land of almost breathtaking beauty or of savage poverty; a land of screaming ghosts or of sun-flung possibilities; a land of inviting warmth or of desperate drought. How you see a country depends on whether you are driving through it, or living in it.

How you see a country depends on whether or not you can leave it, if you have to.

The windows of the pickup were rolled down because we, in common with everyone else in this part of the world, were jealous of every drop of fuel we spent. And, under these circumstances, air-conditioning (like the exorcism of war memories and the act of writing about it) was an unpardonable self-indulgence. K had gone quiet and the muscle at the back of his jaw had begun to quiver. Air-conditioning ices memories with its blandness, but with the windows wound down the past came rushing back at K. "Do you smell that?" he asked me more than once, looking at me as if expecting to see the same war-shocked look on my face as he wore on his own. I nodded. But what I was smelling was not what K was smelling. I was smelling now, he was smelling memories.

Places have their own peculiar smells, and here in Murewa the smell was sun on hot rocks (it was a valley stretched between vast erupting kopjes that look like hundred-foot-high boils); it was the nose-stung scent of goats (even back in the seventies, when K was a troopie here on his way to Mozambique, this agriculturally marginal land had been given to the Africans and their small herds of goats, donkeys, a few cattle); it was the smell of Africans, which is soil-on-skin, sun-on-skin, wood smoke, and the tinny smell of fresh sweat; it was the smell of home-brewed beer and burned chicken feathers and kicked-up dust.

It is not a romantic smell. It is not the smell of free people, living as they would choose. Rather, it is the smell of people who labor, strain, and toil for every drop of sustenance their body receives from the earth. It is the smell of people who have been marginalized and disempowered and forgotten. It is the smell of people without a voice in a world where only the loud are fed. It is the smell of people who are alive only because they are cunning, ingenious, and endlessly resourceful. In theory they are "peasants." In practice they are brilliantly versed in the skill of surviving.

Dad once said to me, "When the world goes tits up and we're back to square one, I'd bet my money on these buggers surviving. Your bally Wall Street fundi would last about half a day out here before he stubbed a toe and keeled over."

In the strung-out fields along the road, the maize was stunted from lack of rain and had started to produce sickly, thin ears of corn. The cattle churned mud in almost parched water holes. If this was the end of the rainy season, I dreaded to think what October would look like.

"You know what fear smells like," said K suddenly. "It's unmistakable, hey? And munt fear smells different from honky fear. When a munt is shitting himself, it's the smell of onions, have you ever noticed that? A scared honky smells like sweet cheese. But it's all from the same place. All fear is . . . fear—it's the smell of discharged adrenaline." Then K hauled on the steering wheel so that for a few breathtaking moments we lunged from one side of the road to the other. He laughed and said, "You know that rush? Hey? Was that a rush?"

"Yes," I said emphatically, not keen to repeat the experiment.

"*That's* the feeling you get when the first shot is fired," said K. "Ah."

"You think, This is fucking it, and everything is incredibly slowed down so it seems like you are taking half an hour to look over each shoulder and make sure the men are with you, and you're looking to see if they've had their jolt of adrenaline and trying to time it so that everyone's rush is at the same time. Then you shout, 'Go!' when they've *just* got that rush. That's the difference between a good leader and a lousy leader. It's knowing when everyone's ready to do it. . . ."

Two children standing by the side of the road hooted after

us, "Wa-wa-wa!" Their sharp voices caught like gravel on the rise of hot air and tumbled onto our laps.

"If you leave it too long," K said, "then the rush is over. Then all you get is a bunch of troopies with shit in their pants, but if you time it right . . ." K was swinging back and forth from the steering wheel and his eyes were shining. "Then the whole lot of you get up out of cover, 'Arghhhh!' and ah, the rush. . . . You don't feel a fucking thing, you just, 'Arghhhh!' You know? You have this noise coming out of your throat and you're not think-ing about anything except killing. And I don't mean you want to kill, but it's the opposite of being killed yourself, so you're running straight for the gooks and trying to keep steady enough and the gun is like this extension of yourself and . . . That's why I'm deaf in this ear"—K pulled at his left earlobe—"be-cause you're running through the bush firing away and the guy to your left, his discharge is going off right in your ear, and you're just trying to slow everything down enough to get a de-cent shot. And you know what saved us?"

"No," I said.

"Munts can't shoot straight. That's what saved us. They had shitty training and they're sent out to the middle of no-where with half the food and half the equipment we had and their guns were hopeless. Mind you, a munt can go twice as far on half as much as we could. We could maybe make it . . . what . . . three days out there without water. A munt could go five. And a munt could walk—I've seen one-legged munts dragging themselves out of the bush for ten, twelve, eighteen ks. Look at these guys," said K, waving into the unkind land that uncoiled into the great swells of barren, picturesque rock. "They had an advantage in the bush, because there's nothing tougher than a munt. There just isn't. But when it came to a contact—we just blasted them out of the shateen. They didn't have a prayer. We were better trained, better equipped."

K held an imaginary gun out of his window and aimed at a teenager lounging under a mango tree. "Click. Shoot. *Waka.* One time. All of a sardine, dead gook."

I took a deep breath. "How many people did you kill?" I asked.

K went quiet for a long time. Then he said, "When I was demobbed they gave us therapy. Half an hour with the shrink. What is that? Six minutes for every year I was in the bush. Three minutes for every person whose eyes I looked into before I pulled the trigger.

"The guy asked me, 'Do you feel remorse for all the people you killed?'

"I told him, 'I was just doing my job. No, sir, I feel no remorse.'

"Then he asked, 'How many people did you kill?'

"I said, 'As many as I could, sir.'

"He said, 'You must be repressing your feelings.'

"I told him, 'Fuck you, sir!'

"He said, 'You killed a lot of people. You killed civilians.'

"I said, 'Sir, there was a war on, people got in the way.'"

K stared out the window. An unraveling mural of rural African life flashed outside.

Suddenly K said, "I have to tell you this." His jaw bunched hard. "This was something . . . I haven't talked about this . . ."

When I turned on my tape recorder he shook his head and I turned it off again.

K looked distant—the way that a familiar view can suddenly become hazed and remote with smoke or dust. Suddenly he leaned over to my side of the cab and smudged my cheek with briny lips. "There," he said. "Now I've kissed you. Because when I tell you this . . ."

He didn't talk for a few minutes and then he started to cry. I said, "You don't have to tell me," but I was lying. I felt somehow that if I knew this one secret about K—this one, great, untold story—then everything else about him would become clear and I could label him and write him into coherence. And then I would know what I was doing here and how I had arrived here and I'd know more about who *I* was.

K said, "You're the only person I would ever trust with this story."

My heart plunged. I wanted his story, but I didn't want his trust. And now I could tell that K's story wasn't something I wanted to carry with me back into my other life. Into the life-as-mother, life-as-wife. The insistently bright, loudly optimistic life that was my *real* life.

"We were in the Darwin area," said K, and he nodded across the kopje-dotted valley toward the west, "and we had been sitting up on a kopje all day watching a village. I was a lance-jack by then, so it was me and the three ous I was commanding. Two of them were just kids. You could still see where their necks were white, where they'd just had their hair cut. They were just laaities out of school. And they were shit scared and jumpy as rabbits. I said to them, 'Don't worry. Trust me.'

"But I could tell the kids weren't convinced.

"I said, 'I promise you I am not going to send you chaps home in a body bag. But we still need to get the job done,' and I pointed down into the village.

"There was a lot of woman activity around the huts, which is unusual because it was cropping time and they should have been in the fields.

"I said, 'I'm telling you, those women are cooking for gooks. *Let's we go.* We'll find out where the gooks are. Then, waka-waka, dead gondies. Home in time for tea, hey? Come. Follow me.'

"So we went down into the village and we went into a hut with the most smoke coming from it. There were three women sitting there with three huge pots of food.

"We asked them, 'Who is this food for?'

"They said, 'It's for the kids.'

"I kicked one of the pots of food over. I said, 'You fucking savages never feed your kids. You're feeding gooks.'"

Then K said nothing for a long time and he was driving with one hand. The other hand was clapped over his mouth.

I looked out my window. The black-blue shadow of our racing truck humped and bucked over the red ground. Beyond that were huts lightly scabbed with peeling mud, goats (always goats) and chickens and the odd haunted dog. Around the huts, there were children who stared at us with a mixture of curiosity and hunger that translates, in any language, to wide eyes and distended bellies. A single elderly man perched on a stool in the shade of a leaning mango tree. He was as fragile as wood smoke, barely a memory against the landscape. There were young men pushing bikes and herding oxen. But the women were hidden back against the maize fields. They were the bent, solitary figures, jabbing away at the earth with hoes, their backs swollen with the tiny shape of bundled babies.

At last K spoke again. "A woman is incredibly resistant to pain," he said, "and they are incredibly strong. A man . . . you can get him to talk by beating him"—K pressed his lips out to show how easy it is to get a man to talk—"but women . . . you have to use your psychology.

"So I looked at the women in the hut. There was an old woman, a grandmother. Then there was a woman who must have been about thirty. Then a young girl, I suppose she must have been sixteen or seventeen. I pointed to her—the young girl. I told the guys, 'Take her outside.'

"They took her outside.

"I told them, 'The usual treatment.'

"So, they stripped off her clothes and beat her by her breasts"—K leaned over and grabbed the skin under my arms—"and they hit her ribs right there," he said. He let go of my skin; the flesh felt bruised and crushed where his fingers had pinched it. He said, "And her shoulders and the soles of her feet. They had taken a sadza stick from the hut to beat her with. The old woman was crying. She had this old, high voice, like the noise a goat makes when you slaughter it. I shut the door of the hut.

"The young girl was squirming away from my men. She was strong, I'm telling you. She was like a snake, all muscle and backbone. One of the ous had to stand on her groin to keep her flat.

"I asked her in Shona, 'Where are they?'

"Because I knew the gooks had to be close by. Fuck, they were probably watching us. The hair was standing up on the back of my neck. Any minute I expected them to open fire on us. The guys I was with . . . they were scared. One of them looked like he was going to start crying.

"And now there was no time for pissing around—I mean, now that we were off the kopje and in the village, we had to find the gooks before they had a chance to find us.

"So I told them, 'Drown her.'

"Because, you know, a munt doesn't like water. So one of the kids stripped off his shirt and dipped it in water and put it over her head. Then one of the other ous punched her in the solar plexus and she sucked in her breath, and the wet shirt stuck in her mouth and she thought she was drowning." K feigned drowning under wet cloth. He caught his breath and flailed, grabbing at the air with both his hands so that the truck rumbled along unpiloted for a moment.

"But still she wouldn't talk. I thought I was going to strangle her. I kept looking over my shoulder, man. I kept expecting to see a gook or ten appearing for lunch.

"So I tell the men, 'Get her to talk, for fuck's sake.'

"Shit! There were four of us and a whole fucking countryside full of *them* and I'm thinking, What have I done? These kids are going to end up in a body bag unless the bitch talks.

"So I left the boys for half an hour. I said, 'Get her to talk. I'll be right back.'

"I start skirting the village, trying to see if I could spot spoor, you know? Gook prints, gook smell. Gook anything. Nothing. So I come back. She still hadn't talked. She still hadn't told us where the gooks were.

"So I told the guys, 'Beat her some more.'

"We beat her feet and her back some more. She wouldn't talk. Instead, she spat on one of the boys. And . . . She was lying there, naked and crying and there's snot everywhere and she's got these fucking welts on her breasts and her ribs and then . . . raises her head and she spits. That's when I saw red, man. I lost control."

K broke suddenly and he was sobbing hard. "I got a pot of sadza from inside. I told the guys to give me the sadza stick and I dipped it in the hot sadza and I dripped the sadza between her legs.

"I said, 'Where are they?' I said, 'If you don't tell me I'll kill you.'

"Man, I could almost smell the fucking gooks.

"The other ous, they're saying, 'Hurry up, man.'

"Because, man, believe me, you don't want to be in the middle of a fucking village when a fight breaks out. You'll get scribbled one time. Plus you'll scribble a hobo of women, children, babies on your way down. . . . It's a train wreck. I wanted to get the info and get the hell out of there.

"So I reckon it's either her—or it's us, plus a whole village. I'm screaming at her, 'Talk to me! If you don't talk, I'll dip this stick in the sadza and shove it into you.'

"She was crying, but she wouldn't say anything.

"So I scooped up a whole spoon of hot sadza. . . . Oh shit! Oh shit! Why? Why did I have to do that? I had the knowledge and the skills and the ability to find the gooks. I could have *smelled* them out. All I had to do is walk out of that village and start walking in ever increasing circles and I would have found them. But I was . . . I was scared and I was so angry by then. We were all going to die because this bitch wouldn't talk.

"That's what I should have done. I should have walked away from her and so what? I would have been plugged. Those kids would have been slotted. Oh well. Better I die than . . ." K drew in a deep breath. "I took a spoonful of hot sadza and I shoved it into her . . . into her . . . you know? And I shoved and kept shoving and by now she was screaming, so I put more sadza in there. . . ." By now, K was talking in winded bursts.

"And she eventually spoke. She eventually told us where they were. They were close, they were hiding nearby. So we went in there, the four of us, and we killed twelve of them. Then the helicopters came and I was so busy with body bags and the adrenaline and taking care of the boys—my ous needed to get out of there, man. We were exhausted.

"And . . . and I forgot about her. I forgot about her. I had wanted to take her into hospital and get her fixed up, but I forgot. And she had run into the shateen to hide and after that we couldn't find her."

K's voice was high and broken. He said, "She died two weeks after from her injuries, she had got an infection. . . ."

"Oh God," I said, swallowing a surge of nausea.

"I didn't need to do that to her. I was an animal. An absolute fucking savage. I had been fighting for so long by then, I had seen so much of what these guys did, I was exhausted. . . ."

And I thought, I *own* this now. This was *my* war too. I had been a small, smug white girl shouting, "We are all Rhodesians and we'll fight through *thickanthin*." I was every bit that woman's murderer. Back then—during the war—I had waved encouragement at the troopies, a thin, childish arm high in the air in a salute of victory, when they dusted past us in their armored lorries with their guns to the ready.

I said, "I had no idea. . . ." But I did. I knew, without really being told out loud, what happened in the war and I knew it was as brutal and indefensible as what I had just heard from K. I just hadn't wanted to know.

"So her family had me up on a manslaughter charge. The commanding officer said I needed to plead insanity. For three days, I had to talk to psychologists, and I have never lied so much in my life. That's what the CO told me to do. He said I had to sound insane. So I told those stupid, waste-of-time shrinks that I needed to drink blood. That I was hungry for blood. I told them . . . lies. They're such a bunch of wee-wees. They wrote in their books and they asked me questions.

"But they were so scared of me. They knew that if they had been in my position they might have done the same thing. They were so shit scared of being who I was."

K wiped his mouth with the back of his hand. "Fuck," he said softly. Then he said, almost with disgust, "It didn't even go to trial. I got off."

"What did they do to you then?"

"They sent me back to barracks for six months. They made me a training officer. I trained boys to be soldiers."

Then K veered off the road and we lunged down a mild bank through the scrubby remains of goat-picked grass until the pickup rocked to a halt under the shade of a stink tree. K switched off the engine and the air sung with the sudden silence of where and who we were.

He said, "I have to go for a walk."

"Okay." I stared out the window at the undulating innocent land. It spread out like a stain; earth and sun and huts as far as I could see, interrupted with the odd kopje. It was a land dotted with goats intent on forage, on cattle intent on water, on birds trying to evade the cruelest part of the hot day. The bones of some long-ago-eaten cow had been left here by the side of the road and had lent a pink outline against the red soil, a barely pressed reminder of an entire beast.

We both got out of the car. K came around to me. He looked as if he had been crying with his whole body. His army green shirt was soaked down the front, his face glistened, his eyes were splintered with thin red veins. He stretched out his arms toward me and I noticed that his hands were shaking. I walked into his arms.

He put his face on my neck and breathed deeply, as if trying to breathe me into himself. I closed my eyes, and I let him rock me. Under the pungent warm shade of that deep green, leafy stink tree, I was inhaled in the embrace of a man whose anger had once spilled into something so hateful and so uncontrollable that it had killed a woman too young to have been as brave and upright and courageous as she was. She was a martyr and K and I were free. More or less free. Never free. Not if we thought about what we had done.

And then K left me, walking up into the shadow of a nearby kopje. I watched him leave and it seemed to me that the heat and fumes of his hatred danced after him. I slung down the way I had been taught as a child, African style, so that haunches hang between spread knees. It's a stance that can be sustained for waiting-hours at a time. I pressed my back into the shade of the tree. My mouth was salty and dry. I pushed the palms of my hands into my eyes until I saw dots, but I could not erase the woman from my mind. And then I cried for a long time, until I was a film of sweat and my mouth was stringy with tears and my throat ached.

"Madam?"

I looked up.

Two children had materialized out of the sun-danced road and sidled up to the pickup. They stared at me shyly, their bellies pressed out at me in greeting.

I wiped my face and said, "Masikatii?"

"Taswera, maswerawo?" they asked.

"Taswera zvedu," I lied.

And we all grunted in recognition of one another.

"Where are you going?" asked the taller child after a respectable pause had allowed us a decent amount of time to stare at one another.

"Mozambique," I said, blowing my nose.

"You are one?"

"No," I said, "we are two." I lit a cigarette and waved it at the flies that had come to feast on my tears and sweat.

The older boy fished at his feet for a dry stalk of grass, which he put to his lips and pretended to light, in imitation of my cigarette. He eyed me sideways, hungrily, and waved his pretend cigarette blade of grass at me. "Fodya? Madam? One stick?"

I shook my head. "You're not enough years. How old are you?"

"Ah come, mummy!" The boy laughed. "I am many years." He pointed to his younger companion, of whom he was obviously guardian.

"No cigarettes."

"Ah, mama."

I stood up. "Okay. I'll give you something to eat. I think there's something for you." I dug into the back of the black tin trunk. K's green peppers, nuts, and wild mushrooms had fermented into a bubbling brown-green stew. The potato chips and beer had survived.

"Hurrah." I emerged victorious. "Here," I said, handing the children four packets of chips.

Then I sat with the children and they tried to pretend that they were not half starved and I tried to pretend that I could not see that this was the first food that had passed their lips for some time. I lit another cigarette. The children finished the chips and licked the packet. Then the older child lifted his eyes to mine and smiled crookedly, and he didn't need to say anything.

I sighed. "Okay," I said, "just quit before it kills you." I handed him a cigarette from the packet and my own cigarette with which to light it.

The child sucked the smoke deep into his lungs and shut his eyes, a transformed smile on his lips.

The smaller child grinned up at me winningly, his lips greased with chips.

"No," I said. "I'm certainly not giving you a bloody cigarette. So don't even try."

I hoped no one was at home feeding chips and cigarettes to *my* children.

WHEN K FINALLY BATTLED his way back through the bush to the car, the children had fallen in a gentle half doze next to the car and I was drinking warm beer.

I asked, "Are you okay?"

He nodded, but I could see from his jumping jaw that he was tense.

K frowned at the pickup. His look made me feel as if I should have been doing something useful with myself in his absence—as if he, in the same circumstances, would have had the vehicle gleaming inside and out by the time of my return. All I had to show for three quarters of an hour of free time was a few cigarette stompies, empty chip packets, a drained beer bottle, and two starving children.

"My friends," I said, pointing a toe at the children.

He nodded.

I said, "Your mushrooms, green peppers, and nuts turned into mushrooms-green-pepper-and-nut wine. The kids ate all the chips."

He said, "I'm not hungry." He walked around the pickup and kicked the tires, and then he said, "We need petrol."

So together we lifted a container of petrol off the back of the pickup. We made a siphon out of a used water bottle, holding it open into the lip of the tank with a licked-open penknife. I held the cut-lipped water bottle and K poured; the liquid throated down into the belly of the pickup. A great wash of the fuel splashed up my wrists and dried in an itchy, oily film.

"Sorry," said K.

"It's okay."

The children roused themselves and offered to pour petrol for us. Their stringy arms would not have held anything much heavier than a very slim dream aloft for long. K's unexpected smile surfaced. He said something in Shona and gave the children a few dollars each and they dissolved back into the bush. He picked up another twenty-liter container and began to pour that into the tank.

"I should just swallow this," he said, watching the last of the pink stream of fuel spill down the throat of the homemade filter. "Then there'd be one less asshole in the world."

Beware of Land Mines
and Speed Guns

Nyamapanda

THE NYAMAPANDA BORDER post was as poetic by name as it was in real life. There was, after the feeling of stagnation that seems to have struck the rest of Zimbabwe, a sense of life and activity and vibrancy here. Bougainvillea wobbled bright blossoms over the dust-rutted road. Small vegetable gardens surged out from the tiniest and least likely patches of spare ground. Cyclists laden with bales of goods pedaled down the road. Cross-border traders, balancing loads of maize meal and soybeans and cooking oil on their heads, haggled loudly in the streets. A herd of schoolchildren in tatty blue uniforms came tripping past, barefoot and exuberant, kicking up dust as they walked.

The fuel station (the only place in the whole of Zimbabwe where we were able to find petrol) held a TOTAL sign in the wrinkled, pink-gray skin of an elephantine baobab tree. Next to that sign, also nailed to the enormous tree, was a marker advertising TOILETS, although, when I investigated, it seemed that the long drops intended to serve that purpose had long since received all the human waste they were designed to contain. I went back to the pickup.

While we filled up our empty containers with petrol, a very old blind woman (she had shrunk to the size of a child and her hair had turned vivid yellow) was led up to the car by her helper (a young, bored-looking boy). Without any difficulty, she extracted money from K, who said, "The Almighty is very specific about this." He added, "Zambian kwacha too."

We had to bribe our way out of Zimbabwe because of the extra fuel we were carrying. Zimbabwe's fuel crisis had become a national emergency, so it was illegal to carry more than a full tank of fuel out of the country's borders—in this area of vast distances and few amenities, it was not only inconvenient but potentially dangerous to have only one tank of petrol at hand. While K negotiated with the customs official (who was threatening to send us back to Harare for police clearance), I sat on the back of the pickup and kept a wary eye on our belongings.

A lorry carrying a load of fertilizer was parked at the border gate, which opened into no-man's-land and from there into Mozambique. I watched as a group of six or seven young men unhurriedly pulled back the tarpaulin that covered the load, sliced several bags, and filled buckets with the spilling white product.

"Thieves!" I shouted and pointed.

The customs official blinked at me lazily and returned to the business at hand, which was negotiating the highest bribe possible from K. The thieves themselves laughed at me. I glanced at the immigration building, where the owner of the lorry was obviously held up under an avalanche of paperwork.

K was now rifling behind the seat of the pickup, where we had stashed our money. I said, "Look at those guys nicking the fertilizer."

K nodded. "Ja."

"If you wait with the car, I'll run inside and find the owner of the lorry. Half his load will be gone by the time he gets back."

K shook his head. "Leave the gondies to thieve from each other," he said. "Now that they've stolen everything they can from the wazungu, they have to pinch from their own kin. Special bloody people, hey? Aren't they? Special."

The customs official received his bribe and accompanied us to the gate, where the gate guard also insisted on a "price to open the border for you, Mister Petrol." So we paid again and—in another process of negotiation I was now too hot and too demoralized to follow—the gate guard paid his cut to the customs agent and to another man (dressed in camouflage fatigues, dark glasses, and tennis shoes, with a gun slung across his belly). During this time the owner of the lorry came out of the immigration building. He was a fat black man, perspiring heavily, and overdressed for the Nyamapanda border post. He was wearing a purple, long-sleeved nylon shirt that gleamed in the sun, thick, black nylon trousers, shiny black cowboy boots, and rows of gold chains that appeared out of the folds of fat at his neck and wrists as if they had been surgically imbedded into his skin.

I leaned out of the window of the car. "Those boys stole from you," I shouted, pointing at the youths who were lounging, without apparent panic, against the wall of a kiosk selling packets of cigarettes and bottles of orange juice.

The owner of the lorry ignored me, but approached the boys, hand extended. The boys counted out money and handed it to the fat man. "Look at that"—I jabbed K in the ribs—"what is going on? He's getting money from the boys that stole from him."

"Read the sign on the door of the pickup," said K in a weary voice.

I craned my neck around and saw the name of a European aid organization emblazoned in blue letters on the white door.

"Welcome to the New Africa," said K.

I WAS INTRODUCED to Mozambique, at least the first hundred kilometers or so, from the point of view of someone who had (in the last three hours) drunk two beers and half a liter of water and had not braved any of the available rest rooms in Nyamapanda. From Nyamapanda through the heart of northwest Mozambique, there was a straight, new road (widely graded on either side) that had all the hallmarks of an aid project. It looked like an elaborate gift, hastily bestowed and incompletely explained. Road signs were impressive for the places they pointed to (declaring grandly EN103 TETE and EN258 SONGO and EN258 ESTIMA), but the distances to these towns were not given.

K, who was last on this patch of earth more than twenty-five years ago, couldn't remember how far it was to the next town either. "I think we bombed it anyway," he said, not very helpfully, "and if we didn't, they did it to themselves."

Until a few years before, this road (the original road, left over from the days of the Portuguese) was so damaged and broken that in the rainy season it could take up to a week to travel fifty miles. It suffered not only from neglect, but from mines, and had to be demined before it could accept traffic. The removed mines left holes in the surface of the already uneven road, which became a mire of craters and ruts as soon as the rains fell. But it wasn't just roads that were mined; arable land, power lines, bridges, railroads, airports, schools, factories, and cattle-dip tanks were mined by both sides during the civil war.

Mozambique had been colonized by the Portuguese in the sixteenth century. In 1752 the Portuguese proclaimed Mozambique their colony and in the same year began to trade in slaves, which by the 1820s accounted for 85 percent of all exports. By 1912, when the diabolical practice was finally stopped, two million people had been shipped out to the sugar plantations of Brazil and Cuba.

Like the rest of Africa, it was not until the early 1960s that the local people were able to exert the kind of pressure on their oppressors for the colonial power to take the threat of insurrection seriously. Until then, the population of Mozambique had been carelessly and brutally exploited for the benefit of Portugal. Peasants were forced to grow cash crops, either on their own smallholdings or on plots owned by Europeans, and the vast majority of the population was subjected to horrific working conditions, including forced labor. The only natives to have any rights of citizenships were the assimilados—the less than 1 percent of the population the Portuguese considered civilized.

The only way for blacks to attain the status of assimilados— which gave them the same civic and political rights as the whites—was to speak Portuguese fluently, abandon their traditional way of life, and hold down a "suitable" job. They were a people caught in a terrible purgatory: striving for trappings of whiteness in a world that was predominantly black but where blackness was treated with staggering disregard and abuse.

The history of Mozambique's wars reads like a synopsis of an idea to end the world, skip the Day of Judgment, and send everyone straight to hell. To be born in that country as a black person prior to 1964 was to enter a world of oppression and misery. To be born a black person in that country from 1964 until 1992 was to be born into a raging, illogical series of wars. To try to understand the events that led to such chaotic misery is a lesson in man's inhumanity to man.

From 1964 to 1974, Frelimo (Frente de Libertação de Mocambique) rebels fought against Portugal for independence, which finally came in 1975. Meanwhile, ZANLA rebels (massing against the Rhodesian government forces) had been using Frelimo camps in Mozambique as launching posts for raids into Rhodesia. The Rhodesian forces came into Mozambique in an effort to quell both Frelimo and ZANLA. To help serve this purpose, they formed Renamo (Mozambique National Resistance)—whose members eventually included disgruntled Frelimo soldiers, Portuguese who had lost their homes and land at independence, and ex–Rhodesian soldiers.

After Mozambique had gained her independence from Portugal in 1975, the Rhodesians continued to fund Renamo, which was now set on overthrowing the Marxist-Leninist government of Samora Machel. In turn, Samora Machel relied on funds and support from the Communist bloc. When Rhodesia gained independence, Renamo was kept alive by the South Africans (who objected to African National Congress camps in Mozambique) as well as by the United States during the 1980s, when President Ronald Reagan's knee-jerk anti-Communist stance appeared to come at any cost to the people whose lives were at stake on the ground.

The civil war in Mozambique finally ended in 1992, soon after the close of the Cold War. By then there had been more than a million military and civilian deaths. An estimated six million Mozambicans had been dislocated and displaced. The savagery reported from both sides was legendary in scope: rape, torture, forced murders, sex slaves—every possible abuse and insult against humankind and nature can be found in the conflict that had exploded on Mozambican soil.

It would be accurate to say that the only thing to come out of the war was some of the most profound misery to be found anywhere on earth. When the war ended, Mozambique was judged by the United Nations to be the poorest country in the world and 1993 statistics showed it, alongside Angola, having the highest infant mortality rate of any country. Land mines contributed significantly to the crippling legacy of the war.

The United Nations initially put the number of mines in postwar Mozambique at two million, but officially revised it down to one million (roughly one land mine for every eighteen people). Before the devastating floods of early 1999 and 2000 (when mines shifted as far as twenty kilometers, and fishermen were catching mines in their nets), it was reported that four people were killed every month by mines. The United Nations estimates that nine thousand Mozambicans have been killed or injured by land mines since 1980. Few maps were made of the mines laid during the civil war, but the entire country contains minefields. The highest concentration of land mines was in its westernmost province, along the Zimbabwean border, where K and I were traveling.

At one time, there was a lively if limited black market trade in signs pilfered from Mozambique that read PERIGO (danger) or HOKOYO CHIMBAMBAIRA (beware of mines), some of which had the added decoration of a skull and crossbones. It wasn't uncommon to see these signs nailed proudly to the doors of some of the best bathrooms in South Africa. These signs replaced the more mundane WARNING: CROSSWINDS, which had been in vogue in the eighties. The result, of course, is that although a few South Africans had all the warning they needed lavatorially speaking, the poor Mozambicans were left even more clueless than they had been before about the location of the potentially fatal flotsam of their recent conflict. In the absence of signs, the locals resorted to marking known minefields or areas with unexploded ordnance (UXO, in the lingo of the war-weary) with red rocks, rocks of any description, or even branches pulled into a line.

I LOOKED OUT the window at the life that struggled on either side of the road. There were villages spread out thin and continuous, beside the road. Nothing looked old and established; it all looked rash, and temporary—something that had been erected out of ruin, with a watchful eye toward the next possible catastrophe. Outside one hut, a woman was scraping at the ground with a hoe. Along the verge, a small boy was herding goats; a man was whipping a donkey that lunged weakly under the heavy and ungraceful weight of an overloaded scotch cart. A woman swayed under a bucket of water, a baby bulging from a cloth sling on her back and a toddler trotting in her wake. Life expectancy in Mozambique was about thirty-five. Given the country's history, that figure seemed miraculously high.

"Why is it," asked Graça Machel, former Mozambique education minister, widow of President Machel, and now the wife of Nelson Mandela, "that the worst of everything that is evil and inhuman is to be found in Africa? What is wrong with us Africans?"

In the 1970s, K had endured five years of war. The experience had left him (as far as I could tell) still tortured, angry, aggressive, lost. While it is impossible, and perhaps useless, to measure one person's war against another's, it is hard to imagine how almost *thirty* years of continuous war have affected the local population of Mozambique; millions of children have grown up knowing nothing but war. For Mozambican youth living and, too often, dying in a sustained, saturated atmosphere of chaos and conflict, the choices were grim. They could either fight (there are no reliable estimates, but it is thought that there were as many as eight to ten thousand child soldiers recruited—some of them kidnapped—during the civil war) or risk life and limb trying to scratch out a perfunctory existence amid the minefields. Girl children who were recruited into the armies and who escaped the fighting were used as sex slaves.

"This was all under martial law when I was here," said K, nodding into the villages. "All these villagers had to clear out during that time. Some of them went to the cities, or across the borders in Malawi, Rhodesia, and so on, but others went and hid in the shateen. We'd come across their little camps. Just a little bush structure—like a tent made out of branches—and maybe, a mile or two away, you'd find where they had cooked their meal for the day. Then they'd walk miles and miles to their gardens—they'd never sleep close to where they ate or grew their crops. And if we found their gardens, we destroyed those too. Those poor buggers. They lived like animals the whole time. When they could, they caught rats and snakes and ate those. They ate roots and leaves and berries. They were starving and shit scared. They were shit scared of us and they were shit scared of the Porks and they were shit scared of the gooks. Then there was always a pretty good chance of standing on an antipersonnel mine. Imagine! One hundred and ten percent shit scared morning, noon, and night."

IN THE FACE of such profound human misery, the trifling fact that I was desperate to find a tree behind which to pee seemed almost unmentionably trite. Nevertheless, I finally drew K's attention to my plight.

"Too many gondies," he said. "They'll see you."

"I'm sure they've seen it before."

"Not a peeing mazungu. At least not a lady."

"I'm sure it won't kill them."

"Okay, okay," K said. "I'll find you a tree."

"It really doesn't have to be a very big tree," I said. "In fact, it doesn't have to be a tree at all. It could be an anthill. A shrub. A pebble. Oh look, you've just driven past another hundred million possible places."

K gazed out at the huts, imperturbably. "Let's just get through this village."

"But as far as I can tell, Mozambique is all one solid village," I protested.

"I'll hurry," said K, stepping on the accelerator.

Which was how we were caught, in the middle of what looked like nowhere (but was actually the town of Changara), by two policemen with a speed gun who were sitting on wooden milking stools on the side of the road.

One of the policemen sauntered up to the car. He was very polite. He showed us the speed gun, of which he was evidently very proud. "You can't excuse this gun," he told us, rather obscurely. "Man he can lie, but not this equipment."

K stared with, what I thought was, unnecessary interest at the machine and then asked—in what I assumed was a deliberate snub to my bladder—to see how it worked.

"No, no," said the policeman. "You can't unless there is a speeding car."

"Well, how many cars come on this road every day?"

The policeman wobbled his head, considering. "Maybe one hundred. Or two."

"How many of those are speeding?"

"If they are foreign," said the policeman slyly, "then it is one hundred. Or two."

"Nice little business," commented K.

The policemen laughed appreciatively. "Come back to where I am sitting with my friend. Let us talk."

"Pay anything," I implored as K got out of the car, "and let's find a place for me to stop."

By now a curious cluster of children had congregated noiselessly around the car. They had approached me crouched, like soldiers, bellying their way over the ground toward the road and making silent "feed me" gestures with cupped hands. I couldn't understand their reticence, until they caught the eye of one of the policemen, who threw himself after them with handfuls of rocks, shrieking at the top of his voice. The children exploded back to the hut from which they had snuck, backs arched in a futile attempt to avoid the barrage of rocks that hailed down on their little bodies.

I turned to the policeman with the beginnings of a protest on my lips, but he cut me off, saying, "Those childs. You know! If you are not looking, even if you *are* looking—they steal even the shirt you are wearing on your body."

K returned to the car and announced that the fine was astonishingly steep and payable only in American dollars, which seemed suspect and I said as much. K said, "I can haggle if you want. But we'll be here for hours."

"Forget it," I said. "Let's just pay and get to the nearest tree."

We're Not Really Lost

Double-story hut—Mozambique

WE TOOK A LEFT turn before Tete, on the road that declared itself (on a grand, green sign) to be leading to towns that we never reached, or if we did, they didn't exist when we got there. We were heading for the area around Wasa Basa Lake. K had a friend in Harare who knew someone by the name of Connor who had a fishing camp on the lake and who had said that he would be willing to let us camp on his premises. When K was a soldier here, the lake had not existed. At that time, the place that the lake now covers was the lower end of the Pepani River. It had been a land of many kopjes, dry and densely covered with mopane woodland. The acid soil gave the air a slightly saline scent.

I can't remember at what point the straight, new aid-donor tar road we were on disintegrated into a dirt track and when, in turn, that dirt track dissolved into something that looked like a footpath. But we were on increasingly rougher tracks, the kind that showed where cattle and goats had been herded but had no tire prints on them. Once or twice, K pulled a tatty piece of paper out of his breast pocket and said, "Would you have said that was a village, or just a cluster of huts?" or "Did that look like a left branch in the road to you?"

I sighed. "This doesn't look like a road to me at all, left branch or not."

"Well, if that *was* a left branch in the road, there's supposed to be a double-story hut somewhere here," said K, peering out into the failing light. He tapped the piece of paper. "That's what it says here in these directions."

"I've never heard of a double-story hut. That's absurd."

"I promise," said K, waving the piece of disintegrating paper at me. "Read my notes."

I felt bruised by the road, battered by the pickup, assaulted by the border post, and incredibly grimy. "Maybe we should just camp right here," I suggested, "before it's too dark to set up our mosquito nets."

"No, no. We must be nearly there," K said.

Evening fell as we drove, and the relative cool of night released into the air the smells of the bush. K shuddered. "Boy, that smell." He turned to me. "That's the smell of being on patrol. Smell that?"

Mostly, I could smell us: two sweaty travelers who have spent too long together in the humid steam of February at low elevations and on bad roads. So I hung my head out the window and took in a lungful of outside air and was rewarded with the fragrant scent of mopane scrub and the chalky smell of dust (the powdery white soil that mopane trees favor).

I said, "It smells like the lowveldt to me."

"Man, and the gun oil and the sweat and the kak." K shook his head. "I'm telling you, you've never smelled people until you've been in the shateen with them for three weeks. We used to hum. Mm-mm. I'm sure the only thing that stopped the gooks from smelling us is that they smelled just as bad themselves."

We drove in silence for a while and then K said, "We were just like the gondies, the way we hid out in the bush and never slept in the same place twice and never ate where we slept. We used to stop, just as it was getting dark, and we made our supper over those little gas stoves that just got the food puke-warm and made everything taste like lighter fluid. We couldn't cook with a fire—the smell of wood smoke carries too far."

"But you smoked cigarettes."

K shrugged. "Ja, we would have died without our cigarettes. We had to have something. But we smoked carefully, hey. Everyone lit up at one time, to limit the amount of time the smoke was in the air. It dissipates quite quickly out here, hey? And it was those old toasted cigarettes—they don't have such a strong smell as those things you buy today that are all chemicals and full of shit."

"Did you ever get attacked at night?"

"Oh ja. Some ous used to sleep in full gear because of that, but not me. Those fart sacks were clammy enough as it was."

We drove along in silence for another half an hour or so. By now, there was no light at all. The brilliant sunset that had speared, in slices of orange and bleeding red, through the mopane trees had turned sullen. There was, as yet, no moon. The mopanes flashed past us, tall as soldiers, briefly illuminated and then shrinking quickly back into the homogeneous oblivion of the world beyond our headlights that sliced through the black world in front of us in two plunging beams. K and I were on a lonely, mad mission. The two of us lurching on an unlikely journey up a lonely road in the dark, thick beginning of a Mozambique night. As our pickup churned over rocks and through thick sand, the engine drowned out the night cries of the cicadas, the crickets, and the nightjars. Behind us, a plume of dust burned pink in our rear lights.

Before complete darkness had fallen, we had caught sun-slurred glimpses of the lake but now it seemed to me that we had veered in a direction likely to take us farther from the lake.

"Do you think we're going in the right general direction?" I tried timidly.

"Of course we are."

"It's just," I went on weakly, "we don't seem to be getting there."

"It's a big country," said K.

"Yes, but we don't need to make it bigger than it already is by driving over every square inch of it." I looked out the window and said, in a carefully casual voice, "We could always stop and ask someone."

K glared at me. "I know this place like the back of my hand," he said. "I've walked all over this land. Shit, I've crawled over half of it on my belly."

We dodged off the track we were on and started to crash our way down something that resembled a goat trail and continued along in this fashion (weaving our way, more or less arbitrarily, it seemed to me, from one narrow path to the next as trees allowed) for another half an hour or so, passing through several villages and, once or twice, narrowly missing an off-guard pedestrian or laboring cyclist.

"Look at all the villagers," I said at last, "who are just waiting for an opportunity to tell us where we are."

So that, at last, K stopped and asked someone, in Shona, where Mr. Connor's camp was, and we set off in a fresh direction with fresh and (as it turns out) misplaced enthusiasm. We drove for over an hour, occasionally feeling and smelling (rather than seeing) that we were closer to the lake (it gusted a brief, damp coolness at us, soaked with a scent of mud and fish).

Then K finally stopped and switched off the engine. Into the ticking silence that followed the relentless hum and whine of the car engine he said, "I have no fucking idea where we are."

WE NEVER DID find our way. It was Connor who eventually found us. We had parked near a double-story hut that had loomed out of the darkness and shone yellow and black, shaggy-haired and strangely reminiscent of something I would associate with China more than Africa.

"Looks like a double-story hut to me," said K, directing the headlamps on the hut and unfolding his piece of paper with the directions on it. "So we should turn left here. Except there's no left turn."

Suddenly, out of the monotonous darkness car lights bore down on us (we were, unusually, on something closer to a road than to a goat track) and a land cruiser slammed to a stop next to us.

"Connor," said a man, climbing out of the land cruiser and extending his hand.

"Oh, what a coincidence! We were just looking for you," I said, employing great restraint not to fling myself upon the man in relief.

"I got a message that there were two wazungu out here. Get lost, did you?"

"No, no. I know this place inside and out," K said. "We're not lost, we were just—"

"Lost," I said loudly.

K tapped his paper. "My directions said to turn off at the double-story hut."

Connor turned and looked at the hut. "Oh, those are all over the place," he said, waving expansively into the nameless, deep bush.

"It looks almost Chinese," I said. "Like a mini thatched pagoda."

"That's exactly what it is," said Connor, "these gondies were sent to China so that the Chinks could teach them how to be gooks. First against the Porks and then against each other."

"Ah."

"All these black limbs," said Connor, making a broad sweeping motion, "from Angola to Moz and Tanzania—they were all trained by the Russkies and the Chinks. Then the wall came down and suddenly no one gave a crap whose side the gondies were on. You could almost feel sorry for the poor bastards. All those years getting help from the Commies or the Yanks and then the Cold War is over and all of a sudden they're on their lonesomes."

I lit a cigarette and offered one to Connor. "No, no," he said, "I quit. Although I don't know why I bothered. It's not like I'm going to live any longer just because I don't smoke."

I said, "We've been driving around the lake for hours."

"*An* hour," corrected K.

Connor laughed. "Ja well," he said cheerfully, "good thing I found you before you went off on any of the side roads here. Mbambaira everywhere."

"Mbambaira?" I said.

"Ja, you know. Potatoes. That's what they call them, potatoes—mbambaira in Shona. It's a joke. It means 'land mines.' Place is riddled with them."

I glared at K.

CONNOR IS GARRULOUS in four languages (he speaks Portuguese, Shona, English, and Makua-Lomwe with ease) with the result that his accent has morphed from a white Zimbabwean accent (known as a Rhodie accent) into something resembling a scramble of black Mozambican and southern European. An energetic, cheerful man in his late thirties, with an insistently bright and pragmatic outlook on life, he seems uniquely suited to an existence on the banks of Wasa Basa. An ability to find a solution to the most crushing problems and an illogically optimistic outlook on the worst of circumstances are two of his most impressive survival skills. Five years before, after his farm in Zimbabwe was taken over, at the implicit encouragement of Zimbabwe's president, by a gang of squatters calling themselves "war veterans" (supposedly of the Rhodesian War), Connor moved here to manage a kapenta-fishing operation.

His house is a tall, dank shed that seems to trap the heat of the day and turn it, by night, into foul-smelling steam. His dining room and kitchen are open-air structures—during the day they are poorly shaded from the stark glare of sun that reflects off the lake; at night they offer no defense against the onslaught of insects that crackle in on brittle wings and sink in mounds of tiny bodies under the lights. The garden is a long lawn set about with trees and flower beds, a bright oasis of cheer against the altogether gloomy buildings.

Connor welcomed us warmly to his home, but regretted he could not feed us. "My maid has knocked off for the night," he said. "But if you want to cook some fish and sadza, I can unlock the pantry for you. I am afraid there aren't shops around here, so we don't have anything out of a tin or a packet."

"It's all right," I said, "we brought food."

I opened a packet of biscuits and some cheese, rescued from the festering tin trunk, and set up a picnic while K unpacked the pickup. I was enjoying the first sip of a cold beer when K emerged from the dark. He looked distraught. "They stole my water bottle and my knife."

"Who?" I asked.

"At the border, it must have been." K glared at me. "You were supposed to be keeping an eye on the back of the pickup."

"I was. I did."

"You were looking at the fertilizer thieves."

"But, I was *sitting* on our katundu. How could anyone have stolen anything from underneath my bottom? I'm sure they're not stolen. Let me help you look."

"Did you have a tarpaulin over everything?" Connor asked.

"It was tied down with rope," said K.

"Eh! In Mozambique. The black limbs of Satan, man. They will steal anything. Anything. I promise you. They can steal like no other people on this earth. It is their special God-given talent. Did you stop anywhere?"

I thought of the police stop and of the children who had sneaked up to the car and of how I had been distracted by my need to pee.

I said, "I am sorry, K."

"I've had that knife and that bottle since the war," K said. He sat down next to me and put his head in his hands. "Fucking gondies. I don't care if they steal my fucking sleeping bag or my tent. But that water bottle and that knife . . ."

He began to tear through our belongings—my bag, his bag, the tin trunk—spilling everything out onto the floor. Connor and I watched in silence. "I am going to go back there and rip their fucking heads off," K growled. His lips looked swollen and murderous. "Fucking savages."

Connor, in a failed attempt to lighten the atmosphere, said, "I caught a pregnant puff adder once and when all the babies were born I thought I'd raise them and keep them to put inside empty briefcases. Then I'd go to Maputo and wipe out a few thieves with them. You see, when the black limbs steal a briefcase they run away from you, sticking their hand in the briefcase as they go, to get the money or whatever you have in there.

Then they throw the briefcase away. Instead of loot, they'd have a puff adder dangling from their fingers. Wouldn't that be great?" Then his face folded back into sobriety. "But the damn puff adder and all her babies escaped." He glanced over his shoulder at the garden and said, carelessly, "They're all out there somewhere."

After K had shaken our clothes and food all over the dining room floor, torn the vehicle apart, and emptied out the back of the pickup, the knife and water bottle were found behind the seat where K had put them for safety. "I swear, I thought I put them in the back," he said, having the grace to look a little sheepish. He sat down with his head in his hands for a few moments, and when he lifted his head he announced solemnly, "That's a message from the Almighty."

"What is?" I said.

K said, "That's the Almighty telling me that I shouldn't go ripping people's heads off until I *know* they've done something wrong."

Connor said, "Oh, I wouldn't go as far as that. Around here, you're pretty safe ripping the head off anything with two legs and a pair of hands, with or without evidence. I've never met such a thieving bunch of bastards in my life as these lot. They'd steal the air from your tires if they could."

IT WAS JUST before midnight when Connor led me to my room, showing the way from the dining room through a thin stand of trees with the aid of a flashlight. There are three small rooms built around the edge of the lake's shore and I was staying in what is known as the Presidential Suite because it has its own shower and toilet (K, who was sleeping in a room to the south of me, had to brave the idea of puff adders to reach his ablutions).

"This was all under water when the floods came two years

ago," Connor said, kicking the door of my room open and revealing a simple cement cubicle with two beds, a sink, and a rickety bedside table. "Place was knee-deep in fish and snakes and frogs and scorps. Helluva mess." A thin orange curtain sagged over the lower end of a screened window. The heat had settled itself like a great, hairy animal into every corner of the room, so it was breathless and stifling. "There," he said. "I'm sure you'll be comfortable."

"Thanks."

"You need to keep the door shut," said Connor, "or the snakes will come in here after the rats. Or the wild cats want to follow the rats *and* the snakes—and then they piss everywhere. Man, this place is solid with wild cats. I don't know why."

Perhaps the pervasive scent of fish in the air might have offered one explanation, but I felt it polite not to give voice to my suspicion. Instead, I thanked Connor for his generosity and watched through the window as his flashlight bobbed back toward the dining room.

The moon, which would be full within the week, pulsed huge and silver in a deep black sky. The lake, black and secret and long, stretched out as far as I could see, joining with the sky in a seamless circle of darkness. I pulled back the mosquito net, climbed onto the sheets, and stretched out to make the most of the flaccid breeze that puffed unreliably through the window. I listened to the calling frogs, the anonymous splashes coming from the lake, the intermittent baying of village dogs, and the shrill sawing of the crickets until sleep came.

IT WASN'T YET DAWN when K materialized next to my bed with a cup of tea.

"Bobo?"

I started out of sleep, battled with the mosquito net, and emerged with heart thumping and ready for flight. "What is it?"

"Good morning."

"Bloody hell. You nearly gave me a heart attack."

"I brought you some tea."

I slumped back against my pillow and looked out the window at the sky, barely smudged gray with dawn. "It's the middle of the night."

"It's five o'clock in the morning."

I groaned and felt around in the gloomy light for the tea. "I feel like I've been through a washing machine," I complained.

"That's what comes of too many beers," K admonished.

"No. It's what comes of not asking for directions and driving over minefields half the night," I said, blowing on my tea.

"Do you want to come for a walk?"

"What? Right now?"

"Ja. Right now."

"Okay. You bring the flashlight and I'll bring the flares." I struggled out of the net and fingered about for my clothes. "It's not very civilized of you not to at least allow me to drink my tea."

"You can bring it with you."

I pulled on some shorts and a T-shirt.

"I couldn't sleep," K said as we made our way out of the camp and headed toward a path that seemed to lead from the lake's shore into the mopane scrub east of us.

"Which does not necessarily mean that no one else shouldn't," I pointed out.

The sun, flat and dispassionate, had begun to filter over the horizon, a careless riot of orange, red, yellow.

"It's going to be a hot one," said K.

A herd of goats came tripping out of the trees and tottered down to the lake, heads bobbing, legs like thin sticks. Behind them, two fat black pigs scowled out at their world. One lay down with a depressed grunt in a smear of smelly black mud, upsetting a cloud of gnats into a swarm above his head.

"As soon as the sun rose," said K, pulling aside a wait-a-bit bush so that I could pass, "the damn mopane flies were out." He was speaking in a slightly louder than necessary, reminiscing voice (one that sounded slightly rehearsed to me, as if he had gone over and over these lines in his head for months, maybe years). "In your eyes, in your ears, in your nose. It was hell. And there was bugger all you could do about it—I mean, you had your gun in one hand and one hand free to clear the bush. You just had to get used to the flies crawling all over your face, or they'd make you crazy."

I pushed the hair and sweat out of my eyes and several mopane flies were wiped to their deaths in the process. "I don't know why you talk about the flies as if they were a plague of the past," I said.

We brushed out into a clearing. The grass was flattened, as if livestock had spent the night here, or there had been wind bursts. Beyond the tips of the trees we could see morning fires belching smoke into the sky and then K suddenly stopped in a way that reminded me of a horse that has smelled or heard something that has put the fear of God into it. "Hear that?" he whispered.

I stopped panting and held my breath. It sounded like an ordinary early morning in Africa to me. Flies buzzed, cockerels crowed, goats bleated, and a chorus of dogs was howling furiously. "What?" I said.

"That."

"I can't hear anything."

"Those fucking dogs," K said. "Fuck. I heard them last night too. They must be everywhere." He turned to me and grabbed my shoulders. "Let's go."

"What? You're spilling my tea."

"Quick."

"They're village dogs."

"Not here, they're not."

We retraced our steps, although this time K did not bother

with the chivalrous formalities of holding aside thorn bushes for me but shoved me ahead of him, like a shield, until we broke out onto the shore of the lake, where we frightened the goats with our sudden and hasty reappearance. K was gasping as if he had just run a great distance. He put his hands on his knees and stared at the ground and then he started to heave.

"Are you all right?"

K nodded. A silver yellow thread of vomit dangled from his mouth. He gagged again.

"Must have been the peanuts in green pepper sauce," I said.

K stood up and wiped his mouth with the back of his hand.

"Why don't you sit down for a bit?" I suggested. "Here, have some tea."

K put up his hand and shook his head. "Nah. No tea."

"This is no time for fasting heroics, fergodsake, drink!"

K took a mouthful of tea, swilled it around, and spat it out into the sand. He rocked heel to toe, toe to heel. It was like watching a tree in a windstorm. Then he licked his lips, which had gone mauve and chalky.

"You okay now?"

"Ja."

"Still queasy?"

K shook his head. "Fucking spook bit me is all."

"Ja."

"Those dogs," said K. "Man, you forget. . . . Those were howling."

"Dogs howl," I pointed out.

K shook his head. "No."

I followed K back to Connor's camp, breaking into a run to keep up with him. Only once we were back in the open-air dining room did K stop breathing as if he had just finished a race.

I said, "Hounds of the Baskervilles stop chasing you?"

K said, "It's not funny."

"Sorry."

K sat for a long time with his arms crossed and his lips tight and drawn. He didn't say anything. Then he said, "Most probably just village dogs, hey?"

"Most definitely village dogs."

"It's been ages since I was here."

"Twenty-five years."

"Twenty-seven."

"Right."

"Dogs only live . . . what?"

"Ten, fourteen years."

"Ja."

"Ja."

"Things change."

"They do."

K leaned forward and ran his finger down my cheek. *"Sheesh.* I think it was the smell of the bush, and the way this land looks and then the dogs. . . . Shame, man. Are you square?"

"Smashing," I said, pulling thorns out of my arms. "And I'm wide awake now."

K laughed. Then he said, "I'm telling you . . . I had a major flashback."

"Bloody hell. I'd say."

"You know I told you, during the war no gondies were supposed to live here. If they were found by the Porks, or if we found them, we culled them." K shook his head. "So they tore down their huts, killed anything they could eat, and they went and hid in the bush. But they must have found they couldn't bring themselves to eat their dogs because those, they just chased them away."

"How awful," I said.

"Ja, so those dogs made huge packs of sixty or so animals, just like wild dogs, and they ran all through here and they ate anything they could catch. And"—K swallowed—"you know, I haven't thought about this—not for years, not until just now. . . .

I had only been in the war three months, maybe less. I still couldn't see very well from the bazooka, you know, when the bloody thing blew up in my face. Anyway, we were over there one evening," said K, pointing to the other side of the lake. "We had already grazed and we were on the move, trying to find a good place to spend the night and suddenly we *feel*—we didn't hear them right away—these *things* closing in on us.

"And then the grass is rustling. For sure, we thought it was bloody gooks. So we all drop, man. And we're all just waiting for the first shot, so we could see where the bastards were.

"And then old Bloodnut—that was our sarge, you know, he had red hair, so we called him Bloodnut—whispers, 'I think we're surrounded. I *feel* surrounded.'

"I say, 'Me too.' But I can't see a thing because my eyes were shit enough as it was during the day but at dusk and in the dark, I was blind as a bat.

"Then Bloodnut sees this pair of yellow eyes looking at him through the grass—it's almost dark by now—and he says, 'It's a fucking jackal.'

"Then suddenly there's this shout, and one of the ous says, '*Imbwas!* Fucking imbwas!'

"It was all these dogs, sixty of them . . . more—all creeping up on us, like lions. The ones at the back were trotting toward us, but the ones closest were crawling on their bellies. It was creepier than a whole herd of gooks, I can tell you that much.

"So Bloodnut says, 'Fuck.'

"And I know what he's thinking. If he opens fire, then every gook within a mile is going to hear us. But the dogs keep coming. So he opens up with the FN, just pa-pa-pa to scare them off and a few of the dogs are scribbled, but the others just keep coming. I mean, there were now fifty dogs, fifty-five, instead of sixty and there are four of us.

"So Bloodnut says to me, 'Fucking let fire, or we're fucked.'

"I start blasting with the bazooka and Bloodnut huzzes a

grenade and the other ous are just letting fly, cha-cha-cha and there are dogs howling—I mean chemering—and bits of dog raining down on us and Bloodnut starts crying. Man, I look over and the guy's whole face is wet, the guy is crying like a baby and I can't tell if he's shitting himself or if he can't stand killing the dogs. But the dogs still keep coming and quickly and some of them are . . . Man, we were kicking at them, shooting them at our feet. And there are more, coming and coming.

"And so Bloodnut shouts that he's going to hit them with napalm. He says, 'Cover me!' So we're still blasting at the dogs that are close and Bloodnut fires one off into the dogs that were farther off. . . . Fuck! The dogs are running through the shateen with their skins burning off—and now they're screaming like humans. It was like they were humans in dog skin. You've never heard anything like it. And then the dogs that were close to us, turn tail and they bareka, man! We could hear them for hours. Hours and hours."

K put his head in his hands. He said, "Ja. I've seen some shit in that war. I've seen some shit. But that was . . ." K was quiet for a long time and then he put back his head and howled, high and long and with so much pain that the hair on my arms stood up. "It was like that. All fucking night."

We Just Don't Know
Where We Are

My bed—Mozambique

LATER THAT MORNING, over a breakfast of eggs and fruit, I asked Connor what other commercial fishing ventures were on the lake. "A whole lot of Zimbabweans came here when Mozambique opened up after the war. But they thought they could fish without a permit and the authorities deported a bunch of them. At one time, hell, there must have been twenty or thirty operations up and down this lake. Now there are a dozen of us, eighteen families at the most. If you include the mad bastards on the islands."

"Who are the mad bastards?"

"Oh, we have a couple of crazy bachelors that live out there," said Connor, waving out into the vague direction of the hazy, sun-glazed lake. "One guy, the munts call him Mapenga. That's what a crazy bastard he is. He used to live a couple of hours away from here by boat, but he's moved to an island a little closer to shore."

The maid came through from the kitchen with a fresh pot of boiling water for tea.

Connor pushed himself away from the table and sighed. "Mapenga's been married three times. I don't know why the first and third marriages didn't work, but the second wife—he shot at her when they'd been married a week, so that was the end of that."

I poured myself more tea and stared out at the lake.

Connor said, "Quite a ladies' man too. There isn't a woman within a few million miles that doesn't fall for that man and I don't know why because he looks like he's been dragged through the shateen backward—"

Suddenly K put down his fork. "What's Mapenga's real name?"

Connor frowned. "Piet Verwoed."

K said, "Shit! I know him! I've known that mad bastard for twenty—no, longer . . . thirty years. Everyone called him Oscar because he behaved like a dog and that was the family dog's name. I think he bit people's ankles when he was a kid." K turned to me. "He used to walk into a bar and point to a woman—didn't matter if she had her arm around an ou—and he'd say, 'She's mine,' and I guarantee he'd walk out with the chick one hundred percent of the time. One hundred percent poke rate." K shook his head. "I'd never do that. I was too shy."

"You were too busy putting people on the floor," I said.

K turned his lips down at me.

Connor frowned. "Do you want to see him? I'd get my foreman to take you to his island in my boat, but he caught a lift with one of the other crazy bachelors to Tete to do some shopping yesterday." Then Connor added, "But I can call Mapenga on the radio if you like. If he's on mainland maybe he'll come around and have a cup of tea."

Mapenga was raised on the radio.

"Are you on mainland? Over," asked Connor.

"Affirmative. Over."

"There's a mate of yours here from Zambia. Over."

"I don't know any fucking Zambians. Over."

Connor laughed helplessly and fingered the handset, embarrassed. "Ja, well, that's Mapenga for you," he said apologetically.

K said, "Give me that radio." He took the handset. "Oscar?"

Silence hissed back.

"Oscar? It's Savage here."

"Who?"

"Savage."

There was another long silence and then the reply came, "Hang five, man. I'm coming there right now. Don't fucking move. Over and out."

"Every now and again," said Connor while we waited, "Mapenga decides he needs silence in his life. So he stops talking for four days, or a week. He doesn't talk to the guys that work for him or any of us. He won't answer his radio. The last time it happened he didn't answer his radio for so long we thought his lion had eaten him. So someone went over to the island to see if he was okay and he was fine. He was just walking around in silence, all by himself. He wouldn't say hello or anything. So the guy that had gone over to check on him came back and reported that Mapenga was just being his usual penga self. Then all of a sudden Mapenga decides he's talking again and he decides he wants company and he'll come over to the mainland and want to have a big party, and everyone else has had enough of him and doesn't want to talk to *him* anymore." Connor shook his head. "He's a lekker guy, but he's mad as hell."

Mapenga looked exactly how you'd expect a man to look who spends his life alone on an island in the middle of a lake in Mozambique with a lion. He had a week or ten days' worth of beard on his face, a torn shirt, scratches up and down his arms and legs, and a deep, raw tan, blending to deep red in his neck. He had vivid blue eyes, deeply creased on the edges with laughter (but the eyes themselves had a worried, restless, haunted look), and a sunburned nose. His smile was sudden and beautiful and careless and came easily. His energy was quick and electric, as if you might be shocked by physical contact with him. He was about five foot ten, powerfully built, and wiry with shoulders that looked coiled and ready for a fight.

K and Mapenga hugged, thumping each other violently on the back. It looked like the meeting of two gladiators. "Fucking bastard!" yelled Mapenga.

"You mad asshole!"

"This bastard," yelled Mapenga, clasping K around the neck in the crook of his elbow, "he tried to kill fucking Father Christmas one year! This one is the maddest bastard I know."

"He deserved it," said K. "The guy had no manners."

"You can't scribble Father Christmas," said Mapenga, "just because he doesn't have manners."

"His kid called my wife a bitch," explained K, "so I punched him."

"And stuffed his beard down his throat," laughed Mapenga.

K said, "I don't fight anymore."

"Bullshit."

"I promise you. I swear it's the truth. I haven't hit someone for a year. Longer maybe."

"Really?" Mapenga stared at K, his mouth open. "Then what the fuck do you do with yourself all day now?"

K laughed.

"Who's this?" said Mapenga turning to me.

I was introduced.

"Do you like to fish?"

"Not really," I admitted.

"Good, you can come and stay on my island then," said Mapenga to K. "She can cook and we'll go fishing. Shit, that will be lekker. You'll come?"

K nodded.

And Mapenga laughed with delight, a surprising noise, like a chicken getting chased around a farmyard.

We packed up a duffel of clothes and some food and Mapenga drove us around the lake to where his boat was tied up. We climbed into the boat and chugged off across the lake to Mapenga's island. The lake is incongruous because it is new (not yet thirty years old) and so it looks as if it is still trying to be land. The tops of kopjes surge from the water, as if gasping for air, and the fingering limbs of dead trees poke eerily up from the watery depths. Storms are known to produce violently bad-tempered waves on this lake, which is also famous for its aggressive crocodiles. The combination has proved to be the end of plenty of fishermen.

"Last year," Mapenga told us, slowing the boat down to a crawl and shouting to be heard above the engine and the wind and the water, "there were some South Africans fishing on the lake and they went out even though there was a storm brewing and, sure enough, their boat got swamped." Mapenga indicated a place farther into the lake. "They were right out there, in the middle. So two of them swam for a tree, but the third guy didn't make it and he drowned. By the time we found the two ous, like baboons clinging to the tree, the drowned guy was gone. And the guys in the tree said they didn't know where he had gone. I said to them, 'Get in the boat. But I'm just telling you miserable fuckers right now that this is the first and last time you will ever ride in my boat and I should probably leave

you in that fucking tree until the vultures come because you deserve to die a shit death.'"

Mapenga turned to K. "What kind of prick lets their mate
drown and then, on top of that, loses the fucking body?"

K shook his head.

"Anyway, the drowned bloke, ja? Well, his widow sends a
message. She says she needs his body for burial. So I go to
Tete—I fucking drive three hours there and back—and I
phone her and I say, 'There is no body.'

"'What do you mean?'

"'He was eaten.'

"And she throws her toys out the playpen. No, she needs the
body to get the guy's life insurance. Please won't I try to find it.
Then she says, 'He had a nice watch. You can keep the watch if
you find him.'

"So I think, What the fuck. Might as well try, and I go out
there for days and days and finally—kudala, lapa side—I find a
little bit of skop floating in the water and a tiny bit of the ou's
backbone, but nothing else. No fucking watch. So I put this lot
in a cooler and I go to Maputo to put it on the plane back to
South Africa and I explain to the immigration guy the long
story, and he looks in his fucking book and he tells me, 'No, the
dead man's visa has expired. He cannot fly.'"

Mapenga starts laughing, his high chicken laugh. "Man! So
I say to the guy, 'That's okay. I'll just leave this cold box here until you can get him another visa,' and I put down the cold box
on his desk and start walking away and he starts hunnering, 'No!
No!' The cold box was on the flight that afternoon, but you
know what pisses me off?"

"What?" asked K.

"The fucking widow didn't even thank me. *And* she's still
got my fucking cold box. It was a bloody good cold box and now
she has it." Mapenga shook his head and pressed the throttle

forward. The boat reared slightly in the water and then began to pulse and smack on the little waves, farther and farther from mainland toward his little speck of island. His island was flatter than some of the other chunks of land that poked up into the air, sloping on the west side into steep cliffs.

"I tell you something," said Mapenga to me, when we had skirted the cliffs with which his island faced the world and arrived at a sandbar upon which the boat was dragged, "you come out here—it's all mad bastards out here. They're reasonably mad on the mainland, but they're madder out here in the middle. The more remote you are, the madder the bastards get."

K jumped out of the boat and tied it to a post. Mapenga said to me, "They call this island Nyama Musha—'village of meat.' It must have been a poacher's camp after the hondo. I've found the odd shell lying around."

WE WALKED UP to Mapenga's house from the boat, past his prehistoric-looking fishing boats with their long, kapenta-reaching arms, past the workshops with their rows of chalk-boards giving instructions for the day to the laborers, and onto a wide patch of lawn. Suddenly a lion, who had been crouching behind a stand of lemongrass, came barreling out from his cover, ducked behind Mapenga's legs, and made straight for me, pouncing from a flat-out run into a soaring attack. I was aware only of something massive and tawny spread-eagled in flight behind me. Before the lion could land on my back, K had caught him with a block to the throat.

The lion was a ten-month-old male, he weighed at least 160 pounds, and every inch of his body was muscle. His paws were bigger, with an inch to spare all around, than the span of my hands. K dropped the lion, and held his foot on the creature's throat, then he grabbed the lion's tail and forced it into his mouth, like a bit. The lion lay panting, its mouth hanging wide to avoid biting his own tail. He grunted in protest and flattened his ears and made a low, snarling noise in the back of his throat.

"None of that, my boy," said K, turning the lion's tail around in his fist, like a rope, and smacking the animal on the nose. The lion looked away. K waited a beat and then stood up. The lion, watching him warily, edged his haunches under him and his tail flicked back and forth. K stood, shoulders square to the lion, facing him in an unequivocal challenge. The lion looked away again and gave itself an embarrassed lick.

"Sheeee-it!" said Mapenga. "I've never seen anyone do that to Mambo before. Ha! And did you see the way my lion is such a clever boy? He went straight for the weakest link," he said, turning to me. "How do you like that? He sensed you were the wee-wee in the group and you were going to be snuffed," and he laughed.

I attached myself as closely as I could to K and we negoti-ated the rest of the journey to the house. The lion tried again and again to insinuate his way past K's legs and launch himself on me, but K roared at him and gave him a hefty kick in the chest and the lion backed down. Mapenga appeared to find the whole episode amusing, chuckling to himself in a high, mad cackle each time the lion attempted an attack.

Mapenga's house consisted of a kitchen and bathroom sur-rounded by a caged-in veranda. "I have to put cages up," Ma-penga explained, "or the lion gets in and chews everything to shreds." He turned to me. "So you'd better sleep in here, or he'll eat you in the night," and again the choke of laughter.

The lion followed us onto the veranda. He was damp and, having played strenuously with his meal that day, he reeked, not only of his own, raucous cat pungency, but also of less-than-fresh catch-of-the-day. Mambo's diet consisted of chunks of whole, skinned crocodiles salvaged from a peculiar accident of tourism at a nearby camp. Apparently, a few miles farther up the lake, fourteen- and sixteen-foot crocodiles had escaped from a breeding tank on a crocodile farm and had found their way into a swimming pool at a nearby guest lodge. The crocodiles had all been shot by the time breakfast had been laid out on the veranda, although the pool was bloodstained by then and there were a few broken windows.

I said, "At least it's not salvaged tourist meat in the deep freeze. Ha, ha." But what had sounded ridiculous and impossible a few days ago was beginning to feel increasingly and fatally likely.

When Mapenga sat down on the sofa, the lion piled on top of him, knocked him over, and began vigorously licking his face and arms.

I sat in a chair as far away from the lion as I could get and lit a cigarette.

K went into the house to wash up. The lion was now standing astride his prostrate owner and taking long, appreciative strokes of Mapenga's neck. "I think he likes the taste of salt from my sweat," Mapenga laughed. "Hey Mambo, my darling boy. Hey Mambo, Mambo." The lion took one of Mapenga's arms in his mouth and chewed on it. "Oh," laughed Mapenga, wiping blood off his hand from a couple of puncture wounds, "he's eating me. Don't eat me Mambo—that hurts."

"Ha," I bleated weakly, and regretted instantly that I had uttered any noise at all.

The lion, who had been entirely focused on his master, abruptly turned his yellow-brown eyes on me. His look went straight through me, down my spine, and hit the soles of my feet. Remembering that animals can smell fear, I puffed furiously on my cigarette, creating what I hoped to be a curtain of odorous smoke between the cat and myself. To no effect. The lion jumped off Mapenga, sauntered past the coffee table, and, rising on his back legs, knocked me flat back in my chair.

"He's just showing you love," laughed Mapenga as my cigarette flew out of my hand and my sunglasses were knocked off my head. "Just push him off," he said as the lion cupped both front paws around the back of my neck and tore my shirtsleeve from shoulder to elbow. "Down, Mambo," said Mapenga as Mambo's dewclaw caught on the back of my neck. "It's only play-play biting."

Once again, K came to my rescue. The lion was plucked off me by the scruff of his neck and pinned to the ground.

"You okay?" K asked me.

I nodded and tried to rearrange what very little was left of my dignity.

"I'm going to put this cat outside," said K. He held the furious lion by the tail and dragged him off the veranda backward. The lion gave a whimpering sort of grunt as he was sent staggering out onto the lawn, and then he rolled onto his side and looked at K with what I could interpret only as a plea for mercy. K wagged his finger at the lion. "Behave yourself, my boy, or you'll learn respect the hard way." The lion laid his ears flat and blinked meekly.

"In the wild, he'd be getting the crap beaten out of him by the other lions," said K to Mapenga. "You need to beat the crap out of him once in a while, or he'll turn around and eat you one day."

"Shit," Mapenga laughed, "I'm not going to beat the crap out of that lion. He's stronger than me. I'm scared of the bastard."

Or Why We Are Here

Mapenga's boat

MAPENGA WAS IN THE Special Branch of the Rhodesian army during the war. "It's where they sent the clever bastards," he said, cracking open a beer and sitting back on his sofa (Mapenga and I were redolent with the stench rubbed onto us by Mambo; K alone still looked and smelled unruffled). "The shit we did."

Mapenga leaned forward and looked into the bottom of my thoughts, his eyes narrowing and direct. He had an unnervingly direct manner and it was impossible to look away from those eyes; intelligent, passionate, mad, piercing. His lips trembled with intensity when he spoke, so that it looked as if he was having a hard time expressing the magnitude of his thoughts. He said, "They taught me well." He smiled suddenly. "I can get anyone to tell me anything. I can get anyone to do anything for me."

I looked away.

"Anything," said Mapenga, sitting back again. "Man, if there was a war crimes tribunal, every damn one of us—from both sides, the gondies weren't any better—we'd *all* be up for murder. We'd all be in jail. War's shit." He lit a cigarette and eyed me through the smoke.

Then Mapenga added, "We didn't choose war. War chose us." He sat for a long time staring at me as if to ensure that this had sunk in. "No one would choose war deliberately. You follow me? But if it's the hand you're dealt, then . . . fuck . . . No one who hasn't gone through it can understand. It's the shittiest thing there is, and the most beautiful thing too." Suddenly his voice relaxed and he looked away. "The only way you can look at it is . . . war's a gift," he said. "It's a shit gift. But it's a gift. I wouldn't be what I am—I wouldn't be living here"—he indicated the cage and beyond that a lawn stretching down to the cliffs that soared into a lip of blue sky above the lake—"if it hadn't been for the war. It taught me about death, but it also taught me about living every single moment to the fullest. When I die and I go up there and Jesus Christ asks me what I did with my life, I'll say to him, 'I hope you have a long time to sit and listen, because do I have a story for you!'" The startling laugh came again. "Fuck! I certainly haven't lived a boring one, hey? No. I've lived four lives—Christ, more." He leaned across to me so that I could see black flecks in his blue eyes, and a small crosshatch of creases in his neck, which joined deeper lines. I could see the pull of sinews in his jaw. "How many fucking bastards in a suit can say that?" he asked.

I looked away and lit a cigarette to distance myself from a sudden sharp ache of longing I had to see my children. I itched for the routine of laundry; the apple-air-conditioned scent of the grocery store; the happy predictability of the days that started with tea and porridge, and children crumpled with sleep, and that ended with bath, books, bed. I longed for that bland quality of domesticity that allowed a creature enough stability to take root. Here, I felt as if I might pick up and blow away from a storm of emotion and intensity.

"You know," said Mapenga suddenly, "I'm square now, hey. But I didn't always used to be square. I used to be really mad." Mapenga looked at K. "We were all mad in that war. Ninety percent of us that got out of that war alive—and I mean the real war, not those bloody pawpaws who spent their time sitting around waiting for a gook to show up, but you and me and the boys who went *after* the gooks—we were all mad. That's why we were so fucking good. You'll find we all did shit in school, but we were great at war. Because we were mad. We're the leaders. We're the leaders of the whole fucking world, but we're mad.

"You know I got treatment, hey? Finally, all those years of hurting people and fucking people up, and three wives, and man . . . I tormented people, but the person I tormented the most was myself. I got in a fight every fucking weekend—it was unavoidable. And my biggest fear was killing someone. I was sure I was going to kill someone and that scared me. I didn't want to kill someone and spend the rest of my life in jail. One night I nearly killed my own brother and that's when my family said to me, 'Look, you either get help, or we won't have anything to do with you.' So I got help. I saw a psychiatrist *and* a psychologist. I drove down to Harare every two weeks for my appointments and I loved it. I finally understood why I was mad.

"They diagnosed me with ADHD—my brain fires too

fast—and after experimenting with Prozac and lithium and this drug and that drug they put me on Ritalin and I am lekker now. I am sorted. Hey. And I've thought of you often"—Mapenga again glanced over at K—"because I think you'll find you have the same disease as me. And Saddam Hussein, and George Bush, and Bin Laden—all these guys—they're fucking brilliant but they're fucking mad. They all have ADHD. Hitler had it, for sure. You'll most probably find Jesus Christ had ADHD."

At which K twitched.

Mapenga leaned forward. "Hey, I heard a rumor you'd gone all happy-clappy now. Is it?"

K nodded.

Mapenga shook his head. "No shit," he said softly, "no fucking shit. And hooch and weed? You don't touch it, hey?"

"No."

"Hey, I respect that," said Mapenga. He lit a cigarette, opened a beer, and laughed. "Cheers anyway, you mad, miserable bastard."

IN THE AFTERNOON, the men went fishing. I barricaded myself against the lion on the veranda and read. Toward four, when all the day's breath had been drawn out of the air, and everything was stung with the need to sleep, Mapenga's cook arrived and jolted me from the gentle doze into which I had been happily slipping. There was a shout of "Mambo! No! No!" and that was followed by a small skirmish between the lion (who had long since grown bored of trying to stare me into a nervous wreck from beyond the cage) and a man in a khaki uniform. I ran to the edge of the cage in time to see a man with a tray dancing around the lion and swiping at the animal.

I hurried around to the door of the cage and stood at the ready to fling it open for the man, who sidestepped quickly across the lawn and slipped in behind me, laughing. I said something very rude about the lion.

The man, still laughing, shook his head. He said in shocked tones, "No, no. It is a good lion. The lion is okay." He told me that it didn't bother him to be pounced on by the lion. Anyway, it kept the island safe. No one wanted to come onto the island because of that lion there, so there was no stealing, no trouble of tsotsis coming from the mainland.

"But it jumps on you," I pointed out.

"Yes, but I have no fear," the man said, "so he will not hurt me. A tsotsi—he will have fear in his heart because he is here with bad thoughts in his head—and so he will die. That lion can only hurt you if you fear it."

I stared out into the garden, where the lion was now launching himself at a jute dummy strung up in a tree for that purpose, and admitted, "I fear it."

"No. You shouldn't be scared," said the man. He paused and then said in a puzzled voice, "Are you a new wife for Mapenga?"

I laughed. "No. No, I'm an old wife for someone else. I am only here to visit."

The man explained, "There have been some wives—or maybe they are girlfriends—who come here and they stay maybe a few months or a year and then they go back somewhere, I don't know. . . . I thought maybe . . ." His voice trailed off.

We introduced ourselves and shook hands. Then I followed Andrew around while he did chores (hacking a chunk of crocodile off a carcass in the deep freeze for the cat, boiling water from the lake for drinking, chopping vegetables, ironing clothes on a table behind the kitchen).

Andrew had worked for Mapenga for some years, he said. Maybe five or six years. Nowadays things were good because the boss was very square. He was not mad anymore. So things were good. Before, yes, the boss had been very crazy. That is why the furniture here was made of iron. Anything made of wood or glass was broken. One time, Andrew said, the boss was so angry that he took everything from the house—including the radio, and cups and plates and sheets, beds and knives, toilet paper and chairs and the engine of the boat—and threw it all in the lake. But what good did that do? Because after that the boss had to sleep on the floor and he only had one set of clothes—what he had been wearing the day he threw everything in the water. And for many days and nights the island was surrounded by fishermen coming to catch shoes and mattresses and whatever else they could salvage from the bottom of the lake. And this also made the boss crazy and he yelled and he screamed, but he had nothing left to throw at the fishermen, so they just stayed there fishing and laughing at him until the engine was found and stripped and dried and was working and he could get in his boat and scare the fishermen away.

I asked what he had done before working for Mapenga. Andrew spat on the iron and thumped it down on a shirt. He was sweating heavily with the effort, and drops of sweat were dropping onto the cloth. "I was just in my village," he said.

"And before that?"

Andrew propped the iron up on its end and stared out at the garden, where the lion was now tossing a crocodile leg into the air and catching it again. "Before that," he said, picking up the iron again and slamming it down hard onto the shirt, "I was fighting."

"For Frelimo?"

"Yes, madam."

"Oh."

Both of us were quiet for some time. Then I said, "Were you fighting in this area?"

"Yes, madam."

I took a deep breath. "Do you know that Mapenga was fighting for the Rhodesians?"

"Yes, madam."

"Perhaps you were fighting each other."

Andrew sighed and stared down at the shirt that he was

now folding neatly. "But, of course." He picked a pair of shorts out of the laundry basket and laid them on the table in place of the shirt. "Yes, there was war for a long time." He took a swipe at the shorts with the iron. "So many, many of us. Everyone who lives here has been fighting. War is no good." The iron hissed and gasped a cloud of steam into Andrew's face. "It's a no-good thing."

"Do you hate them?"

"Who?"

"The people you were fighting."

Andrew frowned. "Why?" he asked. "The war is over. No fighting now." He turned the shorts over and ran the iron over them. "All that fighting for so many years . . ." He shrugged. "Sometime I am there in the shateen and I have even forgotten what is this thing I am fighting for. And then there is somebody who says, 'You are fighting for freedom.' But what does that mean? I fight for freedom." Andrew plucked at the beginning of a hole in the seat of the shorts. "Look at this," he said, showing me the threadbare patch in the offending shorts.

Or showing me the irony of his life, maybe.

The lion suddenly gave a furious roar, abandoned his meal, and threw himself against the cage.

"He wants to play," Andrew said, looking up and laughing. "Go, Mambo! Play with your crocodile."

The lion snarled and scooped his paw under the cage.

Andrew said, "He wants to play with you," and started to laugh again. He folded the shorts, wiped his face with the palm of his hand, and picked up another shirt.

"I know," I said, not laughing.

"Go sit inside," said Andrew kindly. "I'll bring you some tea when I am finished here."

By evening, when K and Mapenga returned from fishing, a strong breeze had picked up off the lake and we were able to sit down at the pavilion overlooking the water. The mosquitoes, we hoped, were being gusted off the lakeside and farther inland. The lion lay placidly on the rocks in front of us, tearing away at his gnawed slab of crocodile. A motorboat chugged into view over the pink-lit water and started to head past Mapenga's island.

"Shit!" yelled Mapenga, leaping to his feet and running toward the cliff, waving his arms above his head. "It's St. Medard. St. Medard! You have to meet this man," he said to K and me. "Jesus, if you think you're fucking crazy, you should see this bastard. I'd forgotten about him when I called you the craziest bastard I knew. This man is the craziest bastard you'll ever meet."

Mapenga danced around on the rocks like a man possessed. "St. Medard, you crazy bastard! Come and have a drink! Come and have a drink!"

St. Medard pulled up on shore and joined us at the pavilion. St. Medard shouted, rather than talked, in a way that required the use of his entire body, so that he jerked and thrashed about and there seemed a very real danger that he would easily set himself, or anyone else, on fire with the end of his convulsing cigarette. "I don't want to see you," he said. "I need to get home." The lion trotted up to greet the visitor, rubbing himself fondly on St. Medard's legs. "Hello, you miserable cat."

"Dop?" asked Mapenga.

"Dop?" replied St. Medard. "Long dop. It's been a shit couple of days."

Mapenga and the lion went up to the house and left K and me alone with St. Medard, who punctuated his ordinary speech with microbursts of hoarse laughter and shouts of, "Mapenga, stop playing with that cat and bring me dop." Hidden under the bluster and the mosaic of coarse, colorful language (English with smatterings of Shona, Afrikaans, and Rhodesian slang), St. Medard had an unmistakably cultivated British accent.

"Where are you from?" I asked when I got a chance.

"Tete."

"Tete?"

"Ja. I've been stuck there for two fucking days."

"No, I don't mean where have you just come from today. I mean, where are you from originally?"

St. Medard eyed me levelly for a moment over the top of his cigarette and then asked, "You're not one of those nosy journalist types, are you?"

"No," I lied.

St. Medard looked out at the lake and cleared his throat uneasily. He didn't say anything else until Mapenga finally arrived with the beers, then said, "Fuck you very much," and swallowed the beer in a few thirsty gulps. He bit the lid off another and gulped that down too. "Ah," he said when he had finished, "that's better."

Two days before, St. Medard had been in a car accident in which four people had been killed. "But I think the death toll is rising," he said, almost choking on a laugh and turning a pale reptilian color that I associate more with geckos than humans.

"What happened?" asked K.

The beer had relaxed St. Medard's tongue. He spoke more easily now. Or perhaps he felt safer talking to K, who was obviously from the same tribe as he was. "Beyond Tete there," he said, addressing himself to the men, "a truck cut the corner and was coming straight for me, on my side of the road. I couldn't get any farther over or I would have been over the cliff, you know. He was going to come straight up the bonnet. I thought, No. Cheerio, chaps. This is it, hey. Curtains for St. Medard.

"But instead of hitting me, he came at me sideways, clipped the side of my cab, then he does this"—St. Medard demonstrated the driver of the other vehicle wrestling the steering wheel violently from one side to the other—"and he flipped the thing arse over tit." St. Medard flicked his cigarette off the pavilion wall and lit another one. "Then his vehicle rolls—squashed. My cab has a bloody face job. But his pickup hits an anthill on its way over, and it's an old hill that's been taken over

by a nest of bees. Then the sports began! Ha! Let the games begin! I didn't get out of the cab. Well, I got out and I got horned
about thirty times in fifty seconds. I didn't even look at the
damage on the cab. I shot back in and shut the windows."

St. Medard shook his head. "These ous from the other vehicle—there must have been about thirty of them sitting in the
back when the thing rolled over—were deezcring. I mean, the
lame and injured—forget about the pain and the dying—when
the bees started, everyone was running. Ha! Ha! The lame shall
walk, the dead shall rise again—that's what it was like.

"Some of those ous were covered. When those bees smelled
blood they must have thought, No, there's a serious problem
here. I've never seen it like that. It must have been a size colony
because you've got thirty or forty munts running in all directions,
all covered with bees, hollering." St. Medard took off across the
pavilion to demonstrate, lifting his knees in the high step,
swiping his ears, and roaring. The exercise left him breathless
and a bit shaky, so he lit another cigarette. "Then they tried to
get in the cab with me! I was slapping hard, hey. I was shouting, 'You're not getting anywhere near me covered with bees.'

"I was stuck in the cab for five hours with the window up. I
couldn't get out to fix the damage because of the bees. In this
heat, hey. It makes a chap lonely for a beer. And I think I killed
Connor's foreman—I was giving him a lift into town when the
crash happened and ay, he didn't look too lively when I dropped
him off at the hospital, poor ou. Connor isn't going to be very
pleased with me."

Mapenga disappeared again to check on supper. I asked St.
Medard how long he had been in Mozambique. His manner
suddenly became shifty and imprecise again, as if he hoped that
by swallowing his words into his enormous ginger-gray beard,
he could scramble his answers. "Thirty years," he told me.

"Thirty years?"

"Thirteen." He took a pull off his cigarette. "Or eight. Ten."
He shrugged. "After the hondo anyway," he said obscurely.

I suspected then that he had been a soldier of fortune, spilling from the Rhodesian War to other wars that had erupted in
surrounding countries.

St. Medard, of anyone I had ever met in my life, was the
person least afraid of death, or maybe the least afraid of losing
life—which might amount to the same thing. It seemed to me
that he had become numbed to violence, accustomed to horror.
He expected the worst from life, and the worst was delivered. As
a result, he looked much older than his forty-seven years: a beer
belly stretched over powerful, stout legs, his beard was grizzled,
and his skin looked oxygen-deprived. But he was, I had no doubt,
still terrifyingly strong and robust. His visible body, abused and
shattered and alcohol-soaked, was the shell within which a powerful memory of survival—a kind of wild intuition and an ability to seek out weakness in others—burned strong. St. Medard
had a special gift that allowed him to continue living against all
odds, even while others died like flies around him.

Mapenga came down from the kitchen. "I've asked Andrew
to make steak for us," he said.

"No, Mapenga," K said. "Not for me, hey. I don't graze
nyama anymore." He looked at me. "Neither does she."

I said, "That's okay, really. I'll be fine. I don't want to put
anyone to any trouble. I don't need supper."

Mapenga stared at me. "You don't eat meat." He looked at
K. "Not even you?"

K shook his head. "It's a fast," he explained.

"A fast what?" asked St. Medard.

"*A* fast," explained K. "When you give up eating something
for religious purposes or something."

St. Medard shook his head and blew out a cloud of smoke.
"What's fast about that? Seems slow to me." His laugh erupted

from the bottom of his lungs and tore at his throat until it shook his cheeks a mottled shade of purple.

"And you," said Mapenga, "what's your excuse?"

My vegetarianism suddenly seemed strident and self-indulgent in a country where the opportunity to eat a whole rat is, for a great percentage of the population, a rare treat. Out here the threshold for insanity and murder is high, but the tolerance for anyone who could be perceived as sanctimonious is zero. I tried hard to think of the best way to boil down the reason for my fourteen-year-long rejection of meat, in a way that would be least likely to lead to my automatic crucifixion. "I won't eat anything that I wouldn't, in theory at least, have the guts to kill myself," I said lamely.

There was an appalled silence. St. Medard broke it. "Well, shit," he said at last, "I hope no one expects me to eat all those gondies in Tete." And he burst into a hail of choking laughter.

Another round of drinks was brought from the house. Talk turned to fishing. St. Medard said he would take K fishing the next day, if he liked, but he didn't want to fish with Mapenga. "He's too restless. You park in one spot, switch off the engine, and about five seconds later Mapenga says, 'There's no fish, here. Come, let's move.'" St. Medard looked at his friend. "I am not going fishing with you, Mapenga. That's flat."

"We'll give him double doses of his medication to calm him down," K suggested.

Mapenga started laughing. "Ja, once I told St. Medard he has exactly the same problem as me. He's ADHD for sure. So when I went to see my psychiatrist in Harare I told him, 'Listen, man, I have a friend who needs the same stuff as me. Can you give me some extra?' So the doc gives me extra and I give St. Medard a month's supply of Ritalin." Mapenga paused. "Ja well, the mad bastard took the whole lot in two days. Thirty Ritalin in two days."

"That's terrible stuff," said St. Medard. "The more pills I

took, the worse I felt. I didn't sleep for days. I was walking up the walls, man. It started out like this—I took a pill and I waited half an hour and I didn't feel any calmer, no different than usual, so I took six or seven and then I felt worse, so I took another ten and then I felt really kak and before I knew it I'd taken all the pills and I've never felt so mad in my life. Horrible stuff, that."

It became obvious, at least to me, as the evening wore on that the four of us, and the lion, were going to be stuck on the island together for the night. The sun had set long ago and had wrapped up what was left of the daylight with an impatient flourish, like someone folding up a picnic blanket at the end of the day. And even had there still been enough light (the moon was waxing nightly), St. Medard now looked far from sober enough to negotiate the passage back to his island, which was apparently an hour or two from here. And still we had not eaten.

"I'm not staying for supper," said St. Medard, less than distinctly. "Can't remember the last time I ate a fucking vegetable and I'm sure as hell not going to start now."

More drinks were brought from the house. The breeze died down and mosquitoes sighed out of the grass and whined around our ankles. I decided to take my chances with the lion, who was perched up on the pavilion wall and who seemed momentarily distracted by his hunk of crocodile, rather than risk the certain deadliness of Mozambican malaria, and fled to the cage. K and I were being billeted in single beds along the wall of the house behind the cage, like soldiers or children at boarding school. Mapenga had said that he would sleep in the pavilion with the lion.

I sat on my bed under a mosquito net straining my eyes to read in the undulating light of a single bulb that gleamed out from the kitchen. I could hear shouts from the pavilion, and gusts of laughter. The lion, obviously missing my company, sauntered up to the outside of the cage and settled down on his belly, head on his paws, to watch me. His lips were greasy. The tip of his tail twitched.

It was close to midnight by the time we ate. K said grace, which was wasted on everyone else. St. Medard looked as if he was approaching alcoholic collapse. He swayed over his plate blearily and occasionally took swipes with his fork at the food, some of which made it into his mouth, but most of which ended up in his beard. Mapenga was sounding insistent and argumentative about something—or perhaps a series of things. Whatever it was, Mapenga was right about it and everyone else was wrong. K ate steadily, calmly. Andrew had cooked an extraordinarily good vegetable curry, although it was harder to appreciate the meal than it otherwise might have been because, aside from everything else, it was impossible to escape the clammy, ever present odor of rotting crocodile flesh (the generator-run deep freeze was obviously incapable of keeping several full-grown crocodiles fresh).

St. Medard wiped his plate clean with a slice of bread and then gave a soggy hiccup.

"That's the thing you fuckers don't understand," Mapenga was saying, jabbing his fork at K. "Because people are afraid to see the truth . . ."

Suddenly, St. Medard pushed his plate away, wiped his mouth with the back of his hand, and said, "Right. I've had enough of this. You!" He hooked his finger under Mapenga's collar. "I've had enough of your shit. You're talking shit."

Mapenga blinked with surprise, then got quickly to his feet. His chair crashed to the floor. He grabbed St. Medard by the beard. "Fuck you."

"Let's go."

The two men supported each other unsteadily out of the cage. They were swearing loudly as they crashed past the kitchen, through the swing door, and out on the lawn.

Andrew came to clear the plates.

K was picking his teeth discreetly with his penknife.

Andrew asked if I'd like some fruit for pudding.

St. Medard suddenly lunged into view on the lawn with Mapenga's head gripped in the crook of his elbow. Both men gleamed in the light of the fat silver moon. Between here and there, they had somehow managed to shed every last stitch of clothing.

"No fruit for me, thanks," said K.

"Madam?"

"What? Ah. No, thanks Andrew. That was delicious."

"You fucking bastard!" came a shout from the lawn.

St. Medard sailed into our range of vision again, followed by the lion. There was a roar from Mapenga. The lion ducked and slinked into the shrubbery.

"Tea or coffee, boss?"

"No thanks."

"Arghhhh!" Mapenga's face staggered toward the cage, followed, after what seemed like a pause, by the rest of his body. He hit the cage, spun, and crouched, and his arms were spread-eagled for balance. His back and shoulders were strung with muscle over bone. He swayed back and forth on his hips, like a sailor on a rolling deck, and then he sank lower before catapulting himself at St. Medard, feet first.

If this was the man at fifty, and drunk, I'd have hated to be on the receiving end of him thirty years ago, drunk or not.

"Well, I think I'll go to bed," said K. "Good night."

I pointed to the lawn. "Should we . . . ?"

"Fuck them."

Andrew brought me tea. "Thank you, Andrew."

St. Medard made a sound like someone had abruptly let the air out of him.

"Good night, madam."

"Good night, Andrew."

I took my tea to bed. Andrew glided off the veranda and past the pool of light that gleamed out from the house and disappeared into the darkness. I changed quickly into my nightdress, then sat up under my mosquito net peering out onto the lawn at the occasional flashes of flesh that hurled, spun, or staggered into view. Within five minutes the men were clutched around each other's necks, breathless and speechless, completely spent. The lion trotted out of the shadows and started rubbing against their legs, purring resoundingly. There was a period of backslapping and a few indistinct terms of endearment were thrown about: "I fucking love you, you miserable cunt."

"I fucking love you too."

Then the generator throbbed to a halt and darkness licked from the deep, African night into the cage. I lay down and held my breath.

"Are you asleep?" asked K from down the veranda.

"No."

"Are you scared?"

"No."

"Do you need to come in here with me?"

"No."

"I'm here if you need me."

I shut my eyes tightly and tried to unpick the thoughts and actions that had landed me here, so that I might retrace my steps back to wherever it was I had left off a perfectly safe platform and dived into the space that resulted in this free fall into insanity.

St. Medard came stumbling back onto the veranda, brushing past my bed. I heard him crashing about on the east side of the cage and then the skid of metal legs against concrete as he collapsed, muttering to himself, on the sofa. Within a minute or two he was snoring loudly. There was half an hour of relative peace, if one could ignore the snoring. And then, quite suddenly, St. Medard screamed.

I sat up. "What's the matter?"

K got out of bed. "Hey, man!"

There was no reply from the sofa.

K said, "What the fuck is the matter with you, man?"

A string of obscenities flew from the sofa.

K came back to bed. "He's fast asleep," he said.

"He sounds like a bloody army at war with itself."

"Welcome to St. Medard's spooks," said K.

A kapenta boat chugged out past the island. I heard the engine, the watery throb and roar of it and the fishermen shouting to one another. I propped myself up on my elbows and looked out at the lake and saw the boat sliding along the gleaming trail of the moon's reflection. A tall man was silhouetted on the bow, a lean figure standing alone with the moon licking his skin silver-edged. I watched until the boat melted behind the corner.

Eventually, I went to sleep, but was woken up an hour or so later by St. Medard shouting, this time in terror. This was followed by wracked sobbing. Then the whole cycle of war dreams started again with a series of battle cries. Soon I heard K getting dressed, and he let himself out of the cage.

I got up to boil water for tea. The sky was only just beginning to pale in the east, the underbelly of day breaking first. I sat on the sofa opposite St. Medard and watched him sleeping, his naked body exposed to a misty and persistent cloud of mosquitoes. K let himself back into the cage and found me.

"Huzzit?" he said.

"They should show videos of this man to kids who think they want to join the army."

"What?"

"Nothing." I held up my cup. "Tea?"

K put up his hand. "No thanks."

"Oh sorry, I forgot."

K sat on an armchair.

St. Medard made a noise like he was choking, a great intake of breath and then a rattling noise, like plates being shaken on a shelf during an earthquake.

"That could have been me right there," said K, staring at the ruined man on the sofa opposite us.

"Could have been any of us."

"Hey?"

"You're your own accident of biology and geography and time. He's his. I'm mine. We all might have been one another but for a minor hiccup of fate."

"This close," agreed K, showing me his thumb and forefinger pressed together to measure the degree of separation.

I took a swallow of tea. "Closer than that." I squinted my eyes and squashed my thumb and finger together. "This close."

St. Medard groaned and slapped his belly.

K shook his head again. "That man will be dead in a year, you watch."

"I don't see why," I said, pressing lumps of powdered milk into my tea. "He'll probably live forever. It's everyone else that will be dead in a year."

Have You Got a Map?

Mapenga and Mambo

MAPENGA CAME TO JOIN US. He sat next to me on the sofa and asked, "Is there tea for me, China?" There was a small swelling on his cheek and a cut above his eye.

I poured a cup for him and he kissed me on the cheek. "Man, it's nice to see a woman around the place." He looked at K. "Especially when you look at the fucking competition. Ha! Ha!" Mapenga took a swallow of tea. "Usually it's just me and the lion. And if I'm lucky I get that bastard for company." Mapenga nodded at the sleeping, monumental ruin in front of us. "Ha!"

K got up noisily.

"Where are you off to, mad bastard?"

"Shower."

"Can't you beat the crap out of my lion first?" asked Mapenga.

"You're still drunk," said K.

"What me? No chance. I just haven't taken my medication yet. Always a bit jumpy until I take my pills."

K left without saying anything.

I lit a cigarette. Mapenga hummed under his breath and put his arm carelessly over my shoulders. The lion came to the edge of the cage and settled down on his belly to watch us.

"Look at that handsome cat," muttered Mapenga. "Just like his owner. Ha, ha!" He lit a cigarette and winked at me. "Hey? Hey?"

I got up and poured more hot water in the teapot.

"Fuck, you people are boring," Mapenga complained, blowing smoke after me. "I'm bored already. What shall we do? What do you want to do today, China?"

I stared at St. Medard, asleep in a fog of hangover, and I thought about the lion.

"Fishing?" he suggested.

"I hate fishing," I said.

"You can tie my bait."

"No thanks."

"Damn," said Mapenga, "that's what all the women say. Ha, ha!"

"There *is* a landmark near here I want to see," I said.

"That's more like it. Come on then. Prepare yourself. It's three feet long. Ha, ha!"

"You know the Train?"

"No one's ever called it that before."

"Mapenga!"

Mapenga looked subdued. "Sorry. I'll be better when I've had my pills. Ja, ja. What train? The mountain?"

"Ja."

"Ja. I know it."

"Let's climb it," I said.

Mapenga crushed out his cigarette. "What?"

"Can we manage in a day?"

"You want to climb the Train? That mountain?" said Mapenga, pointing with his teacup to the east.

I nodded.

"You're fucking madder than I am."

"The exercise will do us good," I said.

"Why the hell do you want to do a thing like that?"

"Just because," I said.

Because I had come to Mozambique to see where K had spent his war and the Train had been a symbol of that war. And because the Train had served as a landmark for both sides of the conflict—the freedom fighters and the Rhodesian forces. And because the Train had hosted a base camp for the freedom fighters until the RLI came along and took it over for themselves. And because I had heard about the Train for years from soldiers who had come out of Mozambique. It was where the helicopters refueled, where the troopies on patrol were resupplied, where numerous battles had been fought. And because, before I had set out on this journey, I thought that I might find the answer to K and to the war and to the splinters in my own psyche at the Train.

Mapenga handed me his cup. "Okay. But only because you suggested it and so now you are officially madder than me and I like to know that there is at least one person who is madder than I am. Otherwise it gets lonely for me here in the asylum. So, we'll climb the Train. But give me another cup of tea first. It's dry out there, I'm telling you."

I poured Mapenga more tea. He lit a cigarette. K came out of the shower, naked but for a towel around his waist.

"We thought we might climb the Train today," I said.

K said nothing. He made himself more hot water and honey.

"You want to do that?" I asked.

"Ja, okay."

St. Medard woke up. It was not quite seven, but the sun had already thrown off any pretense of kindness and had started a relentless attack on the front of the house and he was bathed in a dewy layer of sweat. He sat up like a man coaxed to life by his lungs. He choked and hacked and growled and thumped his chest; the end of his nose went white and his lips went blue. He lit a cigarette and sucked on it desperately until his coughing subsided. Then he caught sight of Mapenga and me.

"Get up to any guava-stretching exercises last night?" he asked.

YOU CAN SEE the Train for a long time before you get to it. A long, low mountain on the other side of the town of Dhakwa, it is a thoroughly distinctive landmark. The closer we drove to it, the more apprehensive K became. I was wedged between K and Mapenga in the front seat, gripping one leg of each man as a way to avoid either hitting my head or being launched through the windscreen. The road was far from predictable and the noise of the engine made speech difficult, so we roared along without speaking. Mapenga drove as if life were something you can pick up on the side of the road for nothing. He seemed to pay no attention to bridges (such as they were) or riverbeds or pigs or villagers or even the road itself but simply hurled the vehicle into the space ahead of us as ferociously as he could. At last he shouted, "There's a game path to the left there. Look out your window and see if you can spot it."

As the foliage whipped past us, K spotted the track and

Mapenga wrenched the pickup around and hurtled off into the bush. The moment we stopped, the heat and the flies settled on us. We walked away from the car. Elephant droppings were scattered around, and there were signs, too, of smaller antelope—duiker and impala perhaps. The land—at least this stretch of it—seemed to have shaken off its legend as a symbol of the war. Now it was just a very densely scrubbed patch of arid ground, silently, impassively allowing us passage—as it had allowed the elephants before us and, almost thirty years ago, K and the men he was trying to kill and the men with whom he killed.

I watched K's back as we walked, my eyes half closed against the persistent annoyance of mopane flies. Mapenga was hurrying ahead of both of us, effortlessly tearing through the bush, as if his skin repelled the thorns. K carried the water. Conversation dried on our tongues. I felt blundering and soft-skinned and breathless. After an hour or so, Mapenga suddenly stopped at some unusual-looking humps of earth and waited for us to catch up. "What do you think?" he asked.

K speculated, "Ammo dumps?"

Mapenga said, "Or mass graves?"

The men exchanged a look I could not read—a look that went back to a time when pacts of silence were made over secrets like these unspeaking heaps of ground.

"The worst thing," said Mapenga, "about it . . . You pour petrol on them and set them alight and their insides come out of their penises."

"Christ," I muttered. "Why?"

Then K said, "Don't ask questions."

"Why?"

"Because there aren't answers," said Mapenga.

"Here," said K, "I want to show you something." He seized my shoulders and spun me around and around. "Close your eyes," he said. "Count to one hundred." Then he let go and he and Mapenga walked away.

"No peeking," said Mapenga.

"You're peeking!" shouted K.

The men started running. Within moments I could no longer hear them. Their footsteps had been engulfed by the indistinct buzzing that made up the chorus of insects and crackling, dry grass. I couldn't see them either. The world had taken on a pale sun-bleached color, shadowless and uniform.

I said, "Ninety-nine, one hundred," opened my eyes, and began to walk.

I couldn't have been more than thirty seconds behind the men, but they were gone. The ground told me nothing. There was no trail—no distinct human trail—to follow. The shallow, glittering earth looked scuffed, but not trodden on. I found myself hurrying toward what I hoped was the Train, but I couldn't tell. Every way I turned, jesse bush stared back at me, implacable and clueless and obscuring any landmarks. I stared up at the sky, but the sun had expanded to fill an indistinct space that might have been perpetual noon. In any case, I hadn't been paying attention to the sun when I left the car.

Within minutes I felt a fist of panic in the top of my belly: I didn't know where I was, I had no water. And I realized that even after all this time with him, I didn't really know K or what he was capable of. I didn't know how intimately he would want me to feel the sensation of being thirsty, alone, hunted.

"Yoohoo," I called weakly.

The world crackled back at me.

I wondered where the nearest water was. I considered sitting down and waiting to see if anyone would come back and find me. The palms of my hands were covered in a chilled film of sweat. PUSHED THE ENVELOPE TOO FAR—that would be my epitaph. Or, CURIOSITY SCRIBBLED THE CAT.

A long time ago, I had supposed that if I walked a mile in K's shoes, I'd understand what he had been through. I had thought that if I walked where he had walked, if I drank from the same septic sludge of water, if I ate nothing all day and smoked a pack of bitter cigarettes, then I'd understand the man better and understand the war better and there would be words that I could write to show that I now understood why that particular African war had created a man like K.

But I already knew that the war hadn't created K. K was what happened when you grew a child from the African soil, taught him an attitude of superiority, persecution, and paranoia, and then gave him a gun and sent him to war in a world he thought of as his own to defend. And when the cease-fire was called and suddenly K was remaindered, there was no way to undo him. And there was no way to undo the vow of every soldier who had knelt on this soil and let his tears mix with the spilled blood of his comrade and who had promised that he would never forget to hate the man—and every man who looked like him—who took the life of his brother.

You can't rewind war. It spools on, and on, and on. Looping and jumping, distorted and cracked with age, and the stories contract until only the nuggets of hatred remain and no one can even remember, or imagine, why the war was organized in the first place.

Suddenly the pale, leafy shrub in front of me exploded. "Waka-waka-waka." The men appeared, spraying me with make-believe bullets from pretend rifles, held at hip level.

"You'd be dead," said K, turning on me and walking away.

"Scribbled," agreed Mapenga, laughing. He saw my face and said, "Were you worried there for a moment? Did you feel lost?"

I smiled weakly.

"We had you in our sights from the start," he said. "We could have shot you anytime." He gave me a kiss. "Hey, cheer up. It's not for real."

We kept walking. It was impossible for me to watch where I was going, since the immediate task of keeping flies out of my eyes and disentangling myself from thorny scrub took up most of my attention. K and Mapenga walked easily and quickly. Both of them, from old habit, looked low and far, where the bush cleared the ground and allowed a few inches of space in which the shadow or legs of a person or animal might be visible. No one spoke.

The heat hounded us. Laughing doves were the only creatures still calling, sounding teasingly like running water. Suddenly, the earth surged skyward and I was forced onto my hands and knees, scrambling and pulling myself up by thick-wristed curls of vine. K and Mapenga were ahead, effortlessly negotiating the steep terrain. About ten meters from the top of the mountain we ran into a band of cliffs. We tottered along the edge of them, trying to finger a way up the chalky surface. Behind us lay Mozambique, bleeding flatly into the lake that shone like a mirage up from the monotonous mopane woodland.

K handed me the water bottle. I drank thirstily. I handed it back to him. He took a sip, swished out his mouth, and spat.

"Well?" he said.

There was nothing to say.

"This is what it was," he said. "This and wondering if you were about to snuff it and become bits of biltong." He put the butt of an imaginary gun on his hip. "Waka-waka." He licked his lips. "Three weeks, sixty pounds of gear, bored to death, and shit scared. That's what war is. Until you're dead."

"Ja." Mapenga found a thin tug of tree that had somehow found a roothold in a thin crevice. He grabbed one of its branches and swung down until he hung over the edge of the mountain, dangling from the tenacious plant that, in turn, clung impossibly into the shallow scrub of earth. Then Mapenga pumped his legs to and fro until his toes caught a grip on the edge of the cliff and he came to rest next to me, like a bird alighting and folding its wings. The sun blistered us against the chalky cliffs. Heat rose and spiraled off the flat expanse of earth below us, kicking up whirls of sand and dead leaves. A Christmas beetle started screaming. Mapenga crumpled clods of chalky earth between his thumb and forefinger and showered the resulting dirt on my feet. K sat down, legs out in front of him. He put his head back against the cliff and shut his eyes. I crouched next to him. We waited. A bateleur eagle rocked above the woodland below us, swinging back and forth silently, watchfully, on the hot air.

"I nicked an ou's water once," said Mapenga softly, throwing a lump of earth off the mountain, so that it sent up little explosions as it fell.

K opened his eyes. "You did what?"

"Worst fucking thing I ever did." Mapenga shook his head. He edged away from us until he was on a very thin slice of ledge, below which the mountain dissolved into a narrow chute. "I was so fucking thirsty I couldn't think about anything else. We had been two nights without water. Now it was the third night. And"—Mapenga took a shallow, shaky breath and started to talk very quickly—"I can still see where the ou was sleeping. I can see everything about that camp to this day. Everyone was asleep, except me. I couldn't fucking sleep. I was so thirsty I couldn't even piss, or I would have drunk my own pee. I was hallucinating water, man. So I crawled out of my wank-sack and fuck . . . I fucking crawled over to an anthill where this ou had left his kit, and I took two sips out of his water bottle. One mouthful I used just to get the cake out of my mouth, that white crap that builds up like fucking cement in your mouth. The next sip, I swallowed."

"Lucky you weren't shot," said K, "I'd have shot you."

"Ja, well."

"That's how I went from troopie to lance-jack," said K.

"How?"

K pointed toward the horizon, away from the lake, where land became an indistinct blue haze and fused into the pale sky.

"I had been in for about nine months and we were out there. Dry season. We were tracking gooks and the sarge had a bee up his arse so we kept going after them and it was drier and drier and I kept telling the sarg, 'We're going to cook out here, sir. We need to hug the hills.'

"And I knew the gooks weren't stupid. They must have had plenty of water with them. We had . . . hardly any. And a munt can go twice the distance on half the water. They're like camels, man.

"I said, 'They know we're tracking them, sir. And they're saving bullets. They're going to just keep walking and we'll just keep walking after them and eventually we'll die of thirst and then they'll come and rumba on our bodies.'

"Anyway, we must have been—I shit you not—at least three days' walk from the last water and the ous run out, the sarge included." K paused. "But I always carried three, four times more than anyone else—you saw my big tin bottle? That thing came with me everywhere. Shit, I didn't care about the extra weight. I was used to carrying the bazooka—so what was an extra three, four liters of water? Anyway, I still had more than half a bottle left. So we're in the middle of it"—K flattened his hand and swept the horizon—"not a fucking drop. We were going to die out there, it's clear. We've walked all day and it's time to graze but the guys can't eat. They're too thirsty.

"Then the sarge checks me. He says, 'Give me your water.'

"I refuse, 'No, sir.'

"He says, 'Soldier, I am ordering you to give me water.'

"'No, sir.'

"'This is a direct order. Give me some water.'

"I say, 'If you touch my water, I will kill you, sir.'

"He stands there. The other guys are watching and I can see they are saying to themselves, 'No, man. This is it. Goffle is going to scribble the sarge.'

"The sarg looks at me and he looks at my water and I can see the old thought process. He's wondering, If I grab his water, is this mad bastard really going to snuff me?

"And I don't know. Maybe I would. Maybe I wouldn't have. I'll never know.

"He says, 'I'll have you for insubordination.'

"I laugh. I tell him, 'Who has the water?' I mean, it seemed to me that whoever had the water was the boss, ja? I say, 'If you'd said "please" I might have considered it.'

"So the sarge, he licks his lips and his tongue is white, you know, like chalk. He says, 'Please?'

"I say, 'Too fucking late for that now, sir.'

"It took us another two days before we found water. I let the other two guys have a sip, but not the sarge. He was the idiot that got us out that far to begin with. And we lost the gooks. Anyway, when we got back to headquarters, the sarge recommended me for a promotion. He told the CO, 'He's too damned headstrong to keep as a troopie.'"

Mapenga gave a noise in the back of his throat, like a laugh. I looked up. He was pressed against the white sash of cliffs. He had taken off his hat, which he held by his side, and his head was thrown back. He was looking at the eagle, which was still sashaying across the sky on the waves of scorched air.

"Ja," he said. "Imagine getting to the point you'd kill someone on your own side for a sip of water. Imagine that. We weren't animals. No animal would behave like we did. We were worse than animals."

Then he dropped off the cliff into the gully below him and for a second it seemed that the heat pressing up from the earth would sustain him in flight. He hung on the pale throb of sunlight, and then the air gave way and he sank and tumbled off the mountain. We could hear the gully rushing behind him, a dry avalanche of rocks and thorn bushes and chunks of cliff.

I stood up.

White clouds of dust kicked up.

K said, "I'm not carrying him out if he sprains an ankle."

"It's his neck I'm thinking about."

"Well, if he breaks his neck, then we leave him for the birds."

I edged over to the gully and peered down it. The earth was settling back over itself. Mapenga had disappeared.

K and I took it in turns skidding down a less steep route. We grabbed rocks and trees and shrubs as handholds. Mapenga was waiting at the bottom, picking his teeth with a stalk of grass and staring at his shoes. "Come on, my Chinas," he said without looking up. "What took you so long?"

"That was fucking stupid," said K, wiping the dust off his lips with the back of his hand.

Mapenga laughed and scrambled to his feet. "Man, I am parched. How does a cold beer sound to me?"

K was already ahead of us, as silent on his feet as an owl is on the wing. He walked like a dancer, deliberate with his feet even while he was apparently unconscious of them.

Mapenga winked at me. "Remember, rule number one of flying."

"What?"

"Don't think about whether it'll kill you or not. Just spread your wings and drop."

I Don't Remember
Getting Here

A road

THE ROADS WE WERE ON, and the towns we were driving through, did not appear on any map. They hadn't been forgotten. They were never remembered in the first place. They were the new Mozambique. If the roads in some countries in the world were built wide enough to accommodate a carriage turning in the street, a presidential entourage, a celebrity's limousine, or a Roman chariot, then these roads were built wide enough to accommodate an army truck—a single army truck bearing down in blind rage from the dizzy height of some remote power to quell a rebellion. Or a food-aid truck sent from the even dizzier heights of ever more remote powers to quell a famine.

"Let me show you some old Mozambique," said Mapenga, suddenly veering off the road and onto something wide enough to allow for a couple of goats. We drove for some distance through a scrubby wasteland of bush, and then suddenly we broke through the scruffy backcountry into a clearing. Here, there was a small, dusty village that had crowded itself around a single, tiny shack serving as a grocery store.

"This used to be a town in Pork days," said Mapenga. "Believe it or not. Nice place, they say. There was a club, and a hardware store, restaurant. Now look."

A single telephone pole leaned against a solitary stone building, which blinked under the relentless sun. Its roof and back wall had been blown off, revealing a cross section of remarkably thick walls. A massive mango tree grew out of one of the windows.

"They arrested me a few years ago and tossed me in there for three nights," said Mapenga. "The usual hunna-hunna about, 'You wazungu think you can come here and do anything.' You know how it is? You fire some lazy bastard and his brother is the local policeman, so they come and arrest you and keep you until they admit they haven't got any evidence against you." Then Mapenga repeated the word with a Shona accent, "Heavy-dents. Ha!

"So I tell the policeman, 'What's stopping me walking out of here?'

"He said, 'We shoot you.'"

Mapenga laughed. "See?" he said, slapping my knee. *"Heavy-dents.* That's what they say. They say, 'That is not a bullet hole. It is a heavy-dent.' Ha! Ha!"

Mapenga changed gears and the engine whined. The pickup lurched into a slower pace. "So for three nights I am stuck on this slab of concrete and there are chickens and kids and dogs wandering in and out and there's a gondie in the mango tree with an AK-47 with the barrel pointing straight at my brain. The kids fetched me burned mealies and water, though. And the guy in the tree with the gun threw mangos down for me once in a while. We became quite good mates. Sometimes I come through here and give him a packet of kapenta."

A group of four or five women standing by the side of the road, with plastic containers and buckets on their heads, shouted and waved as Mapenga drove past. "My girlfriends," he said, winking at K and slamming on the brakes, so that we were enveloped in a cloak of white dust. He reversed the pickup and the women climbed into the back. Mapenga leaned out the window and said something in Shona; they shrieked and laughed in response.

K glanced behind at the women. "The Porks weren't afraid of dipping into the oil drum, hey."

"Plenty of goffles around here," Mapenga agreed. "Beautiful as well. There are some that are almost white, I promise you." Mapenga lit a cigarette. "It's tempting, sometimes. There's a bar in Maputo that I go to where all the prozzies hang out. You know, the classy ones. The ones with Pork blood in them. You've never seen such women. More beautiful than wazungu women, I'm telling you." Mapenga cleared his throat. "Ja, so last month I was there and the owner is the slimiest fucking Pork you've ever met.

"He tells me, 'Hey, Mila is in the back room. She's so drunk. She's giving it away.'

"And Mila, I promise, she's the most beautiful mawhori you've seen. And about eight guys have already been in there and done her." Mapenga shook his head. "Death sentence, man.

"I told the owner, 'No thanks. I've seen plenty of The Very Disease. I don't need to go looking for it.'

"He said, 'No problemo, she's clean.'

"I said, 'If she was clean an hour ago, she certainly isn't now.'"

By now we had cleared the village and we were driving through a surprising and sudden pastoral patch of country. It looked like something torn from a storybook of Europe and laid across the ache of scrub that lay behind us. Great fields of gleaming green grass lay cropped on either side of us, like English meadows. All along the road were herds of cattle, flocks of goats, donkey carts, and a multitude of people; a river of patient life, pressing toward the east, like a pilgrimage. Mapenga slowed the pickup to a crawl and then the crowd was too thick for us to make passage through them. So he stopped the vehicle and we all climbed out, the women who had hitched a ride with us thanking Mapenga with clapping hands.

Now we joined the surge of bodies, along braided paths under an avenue of fragile fir trees that seeped a northern scent into the air. People clucked and sang to their livestock, children suckled and cried, feet and hooves kicked up a billowing atmosphere of manure-scented dust. I found myself shoulder to shoulder with Mapenga on the one side and, on the other, a woman and her child. She had covered her head from the sun with a drape of bright blue-and-red cloth. A flock of goats trotted ahead of her. She was calling to them, or singing to her baby, I couldn't tell which, in a soft, monotonous nasal tone. K was forging ahead like a man accustomed to crossing a sea of humanity and livestock.

Then, quite suddenly, we came to a standstill and the swarm of animals and people arranged themselves into a thick rope that snaked down from a small hill, all the way to a mango orchard that lay below us. Towering up all around us, and providing an almost liquid shade, was an eruption of enormous trees, a vast thicket of lush green.

The place—milling as it was with women, men, children, and livestock—was suddenly strangely silent. Except for the animals complaining softly, and the odd bleat of babies, few people were talking and those who were talked in hushed, reverent tones. Everyone appeared to be waiting for someone or something. The queer peace was broken only by the occasional, high shrill sound of a man yelling and the sharp report of a whip cracking.

Mapenga seized my hand. "Follow me."

We pressed through the crush of cows and people and into a tiny area that looked like an old stone chapel without a roof. K was already standing in front of the chapel walls.

"Look," said Mapenga.

The floor of the chapel was a deep, clear well, echoing its own brilliance back at us, light turquoise layering down to dark indigo, reaching deeper and deeper into the earth until it became a narrow black pinprick of infinity. Straddling above the well, on a great bench provided for the purpose, was a big man in a grubby white undershirt and rolled-up trousers, which were hitched at the waist with a belt made from a strip of inner-tube rubber. He was cracking a huge leather whip above his head and it occasionally stung down on the backs of animals or people who jumped their place in a queue that snaked from here all the way into the heart of the mango orchard behind us.

"Dry season, wet season, year after year, this well never dries up," said Mapenga.

It was a miracle of pure water in a place that was otherwise so thinly blessed. I watched as a woman stooped and filled her buckets, and then, putting her buckets aside, she led her cattle by the nose, one at a time, to drink from the well. Then it was the chance of her goats and her dogs and her children, who fell on their knees next to the lapping animals and scooped water to their mouths in handfuls. And then another woman took her place and the ritual was repeated.

I turned to K. "Did you know about this place during the war?"

K looked sullen. "We never came here," he said shortly.

Mapenga looked at K and laughed. "Lying bastard. The Rhodesians poisoned every well between here and Mukumbura. You mean you came here once, poisoned the thing, and never came back."

"*I* didn't poison it."

"Okay, not you personally," Mapenga agreed, "but the Porks or the Rhodesians did. Someone did, and it wasn't these poor bastards."

K said, "I'll go and wait at the car." He turned and walked back through the crowd to the fir trees.

Mapenga looked after him. "That man needs my pills too, I promise you. Then he'll be square. You too. You should take them too, then we'll all be square." Then he seized my hand and pulled me in the opposite direction, to the front of the queue, until I was standing below the man with the sjambok. Mapenga spoke to the man in Shona and the man, not taking his eyes off the throng in front of him, nodded his head and replied, "Yes, Mapenga. You may go to see." His whip sailed down and then abruptly cracked back, barely glancing the hide of an ox that was about to step into the well. "But not to taste," the man warned.

"Come." Mapenga pressed me ahead of him, around the edge of the well and through a tiny slot in the chapel wall. I crouched on hands and knees to get through the cool, dark passage of stone, which was about six feet long and so narrow that I had to turn sideways in places to force my shoulders through. I landed on a carpet of moss and looked up at pieces of torn sky breaking through a dense roof of foliage. It was like being born into a place beyond the world. Suddenly the noise and dust and heat of the last few days were forgotten. All here was fragrant and soft and whispering. Mapenga helped me to my feet. And there we stood, hand in hand, in the garden of Eden.

We were surrounded by three stone walls, as high as a castle, that reached back to the hill. Inside the belly of the walls, where we stood, was a cultivated garden that had gone beautifully wild. Mint bushes as big as small trees pressed against hedges of rosemary and thyme. A frenzy of tiny white flowers bordered an ancient tangle of passion-fruit creepers. Bright birds swooped and dived from the canopy of heavy-limbed trees that groaned and sawed against their own weight in the mild breeze. Through all this, from a dark hole in the mouth of the hill, a jumping stream bubbled over its rocky banks and set up silver droplets of water.

"There, lovely creature," said Mapenga, kissing my hand. "I've shown you heaven on earth."

I knelt down and pressed my hands into the moss.

"Anyone caught in here gets thrown out of the village," said Mapenga. "And anyone found drinking from here . . ." Mapenga knelt next to me and put his lips close to the stream without drinking. "They're for the chop."

BY THE TIME we arrived back at the cage, the sun had begun its decline into the lake, dragging with it all the day's colors. K went out into the garden to pray. Mapenga and I lay on opposites ends of the sofa and drank a cold beer. Neither of us spoke. When darkness fell, K came in from the garden and sat opposite us. The generator came on and the fan started to whirl the warm air around and around. We didn't bother to switch on the lights, but instead stayed in the darkness until we couldn't see one another at all. Then Mapenga got up and opened a bottle of wine and poured out two glasses.

"Here's to no more spooks," I said.

Mapenga raised his glass.

"I'll have some," said K.

"Are you sure?" I asked.

"Just a small one."

"Okay." I got up and fetched a little glass from the kitchen and poured out a sip for K.

The three of us knocked glasses together.

The lion came to the edge of the cage and flung himself against the wire.

"Look," said Mapenga. "My lion's lonely. He's feeling left out." Then he said, "Let's throw a fish on the fire. We can sit outside with Mambo."

So we took the wine and a tiger fish outside and built a fire and cooked our meal under the stars while the fire spat mopane smoke at us. The lion lay next to Mapenga, contentedly licking fish flesh off the edge of Mapenga's plate, and we talked softly about other nights when we had sat around fires in Africa— with different people—listening to wild lions, or hyenas, or to the deep, singing, anonymous night. Above us the sky tore back in violent, endless beauty, mysterious and unattainable. There is no lid to this earth and there is nothing much fettering us to the ground. Eventually we will die and be wafted back into the universe. Bones to dust. Flesh to ashes. Soul into that infinite mystery.

The cat yawned and fell asleep on Mapenga's feet.

K got up and stretched. "I'm off to bed."

"Me too," I said.

Mapenga held up the wine bottle. "We haven't put this out of its misery yet. Here, give me your glass."

K asked me, "Are you coming?"

"When I've finished this."

"We have an early start in the morning."

"I know."

"Very early."

"Okay." I lit a cigarette. "Good night." I blew smoke into the sky.

K walked around to the swing door and I heard him letting himself into the cage. The lights came on in the house.

The lion started purring. I drank my wine and then I sat with the empty glass between my hands and stared into the fire until it died down into a heap of ashy pink coals. The lights in the house went out. The fishing rigs chugged out for the night's catch, their lights reflecting like bright pearls off the oily-black water. Feeling stiff and sunburned I stretched and got up.

"Thanks for showing me that garden," I said.

"Have some more wine."

"We have an early, early start," I said. "Thanks anyway."

Mapenga put his hand up and caught my waist. "Come here," he said.

So I bent over and kissed him. His lips tasted of salt and wine and cigarettes. "Good night," I said.

"No," he said. "Come here." He stood up and his chin grazed my cheek. He held me in the small of my back. "Come." He led me down to the lake. I glanced over my shoulder at the lion, who was following us slowly, tail wagging, head low and swinging—he looked sedate. "Don't worry about the lion," whispered Mapenga.

"I'm not," I lied.

Now we were standing on a flat rock above the lake. Here, the edge of the island fell sharply into the water.

"Lie down," said Mapenga.

"What?"

"Lie down."

I lay down on the rock.

"On your tummy," said Mapenga.

I rolled over on the warm rock and it was the temperature of blood, flooding the day's heat into my stomach. Mapenga lay down next to me and put his hand over my shoulder. "Look out there," he said softly.

I turned my head. The lion had sauntered out in front of us and was sitting, statuesque, gazing out at the deep night. Beyond the lion, the sky swelled over the lake, reached back again, and touched itself in the water. The world appeared perfectly round, a mirror of itself over and over and over. Mapenga and I were a thin slot of life wedged into the middle of the end of the world. The moon crept out of the lake, tentative and heavy and yellow, stained with heat and age, pieces of it dripping off its side.

"Which way is up?" Mapenga said, his lips touching my ear. "Everywhere you look, you're surrounded."

My arms prickled and I felt suddenly dizzy, too full of the drunken night and of the slow, ponderous moon and the stars and of the heat-soaked day.

"The edge of the world," whispered Mapenga.

I rolled onto my back and Mapenga leaned over me. It was a moment before I could make out his face and then his lips were on mine. We kissed and it was some minutes before I felt the sharp edge of rock against my spine and turned my face away.

I sat up and the lion gave a soft grunt and started to clean himself noisily. I said, "Oh God, I must get to bed."

Then I hurried off the rock, across the lawn, and back into the cage before the lion could get any ideas about ambushing me.

I shut the screen door behind me and I stopped, listening. I sensed immediately that K was not asleep. His breathing was uneven and angry. I brushed my teeth and climbed into bed as quickly and quietly as I could. I lay awake for a while, listening to K's sleeplessness from the other bed, and then I dozed off.

I awoke an hour or two later into the sudden death of a noise, which in this part of Africa is not *silence*, exactly, but more a reduction of something steadying and reassuring and man-made. The generator had been switched off. The startling absence of its companionable throb and the corresponding stillness of the fan's cooling arms above my bed had jolted me awake. I peeled the sheets off my legs and wiped sweat off my forehead.

Then I heard the crash of something being dropped, a sort of intentionally angry noise that felt *directed* toward me, rather than accidental. Then another noise, this time louder. As if something were being bashed to death. The hesitant pale light of a flashlight caught the kitchen window and blinked at me. I felt my way past the gauzy embrace of my mosquito net and groped toward the kitchen. Mambo paced next to me on the other side of the wire, his scrubby flanks brushing the fence, issuing the breathy grunt that male lions have of expressing themselves: "Uh-uh-uh-uh."

"Good boy, Mambo," I told him, not meaning it.

I slipped into the kitchen, where the smell of far-from-fresh crocodile meat was most powerful.

K was hunched over a pile on the floor. His shadow jerked and bulged, gray and enormous on the white wall behind him.

I said, "What are you doing?"

K picked up his bag. It was packed and zipped closed. He wouldn't look at me.

"It's the middle of the night," I said.

"I'm leaving." K turned around. "You can find your own way home," he said. He looked murderous, his lips almost purple and his face indistinct.

I leaned against the wall and crossed my arms.

"Get your new friend to drive you home."

"What's going on?"

He said, "You know what you've done."

I sighed.

"You're godless," K said. Then he added, "And do you know what absolutely terrifies me?" When I didn't reply, he thrust his head out at me and raised his eyebrows. "Huh?"

"No," I said.

"I haven't read my Bible once on this trip," he said. "Not once." He breathed at me heavily.

I said nothing.

"I believed in you," he said. "I trusted you."

K sent his bag crashing out of the kitchen onto the veranda, where it hit the side of the cage and startled the lion.

K came up to where I was and stood above me. He spoke in

such a low, angry voice that it sounded more like he was breathing the words than saying them. "I've destroyed all your tapes, your film. You have nothing about this trip. You have nothing to say about me."

I ducked under his face, sank onto my haunches, and wrapped my arms around my knees. Mambo attacked the cage, trying to paw the duffel bag into life.

"Don't worry. I don't hit women," K said.

I looked up. "I'm not scared."

"You're not worth it."

There was a long silence.

"Evil," said K, dropping down and pressing his mouth close to my face.

Then he got up and pulled some fishing line out of a reel that had been lying near the kitchen sink and bit through it, so that a small piece of gleaming green line snapped back on his lip. He put the reel into his fishing box and slapped the box shut. "You play with men. You know that? You play with men and you play with their feelings and you are going to destroy yourself. You're going to destroy your family."

I stared down at the floor. A line of ants was hurrying from the top of the kitchen table, in long, quivering formation, down the table's leg and into a crack in the cement at my feet. Each ant carried a grain of white sugar in its jaws. K dropped his fishing box on top of the line and the ants swarmed in a frenzy of confusion. I lifted my feet until the orderly line had re-formed.

When K's voice came again it was low, but very distinct. "This place is evil. I can feel the evil all around me. It's like fingers around my neck. That's how much I can feel evil . . . like fingers around my neck."

I said, "I don't know what you're thinking."

K laughed humorlessly. "Don't try that with me."

"Whatever it is, it's likely to be worse than the truth."

"I wasn't born yesterday."

"No," I agreed.

"And you can't write my story. I won't let you write about this."

"It's not up to you what I do."

"Yes it is!" Suddenly K imploded, his face fell in on itself, and his shoulders collapsed. "You fucked him, didn't you? You fucked him!"

I stared at K. I said, "No." But I knew that whatever I said it wouldn't make any difference. K had gone into that place in his head that is beyond reason.

"Then if you didn't fuck him, you . . . you . . . you did something else. I told you," he hissed, "you have nothing to say about me. I've destroyed the interviews. Your film. All of it. You're evil!"

I glanced up at the shelf, where my suitcase lay and in which I had kept my tape recorder and camera, my tapes, film, notes, and my diary. It was open and my stuff lay strewn across the top of it.

K's eyes followed mine and he nodded. "All of it," he repeated.

At that moment I hated K, not for trying to reclaim what he had given me (that I could understand), but for assuming that he could claim what was mine.

We faced each other in the shimmering light of the flashlight. Then he said, threatening, "I'm leaving." But he didn't move.

"It's okay," I said. "Leave if you want." I covered the back of my neck with my hands and rocked back and forth on my heels, curled up completely against K. And against Mapenga and the lion. And against everything these men had ever done and everything they would ever do. And against everything I had ever done and ever would do. I wanted to get off the island and wash their words and their war and their hatred from my head and I wanted to be incurious and content and conventional. I didn't care about the tapes, or the film. I didn't care about K's story or Mapenga's bravado. I didn't care about any of it, because putting their story into words and onto film and tapes had changed nothing. Nothing K and Mapenga had told me, or shown me—and nothing I could ever write about them—could undo the pain of their having been on the planet. Neither could I ever undo what I had wrought.

I said, "I'm sorry."

"What?"

"You're right," I said. "I have nothing to say about you." I stood up and looked at him. "Nothing."

I had shaken loose the ghosts of K's past and he had allowed me into the deepest corners of his closet, not because I am a writer and I wanted to tell his story, but because he had believed himself in love with me and because he had believed that in some very specific way I belonged to him. And in return, I had listened to every word that K had spoken and watched the nuance of his every move, not because I was in love with him, but because I had believed that I wanted to write him into dry pages. It had been an idea based on a lie and on a hope neither of us could fulfill. It had been a broken contract from the start.

An age of quiet spun out in front of us. Even the creatures outside had ceased pulsing and calling, as if the heat of K's anger had rushed out of the room to the world beyond the veranda and stilled the restive frogs, trilling insects, and crying night birds. Sweat gathered in a little stream under my chin and plopped onto the floor between my feet.

He said softly, "You're not what I thought you were."

"No."

Mambo groaned and pressed himself up against the cage, and a rooster from the laborers' village gave a high, warning howl, "Ro-o-o-o-ooooo!"

K said, "It doesn't matter."

"No," I said. "It doesn't."

Because at that moment it seemed to me that who K and I were mattered less than the fact that we were in this together. Two people in a faint pool of light from a dying flashlight beyond which there was darkness, Mambo, an insomniac cockerel, a great stretch of crocodile-rich water, Mozambique, and Africa. And beyond that, a whole, confused world where people like us were doing exactly what we were doing—trying to patch together enough words to make sense of our lives.

Suddenly K's face was level with mine—he was kneeling in front of me—and I could see, by the light of the lamp, that he was crying. Two silver trails, like the gleaming path left on cement by a snail, shone down his cheeks. "Sorry," he said. The tears came out of his eyes in sheets and out of his voice in clouds, making his words blurred and sluggish, like a drunk's. "Shit, I'm so sorry."

I said, "Me too."

A mosquito drifted onto my wrist like a casual piece of fairy dust. I pressed it with my thumb and it left a smudge of blood on my skin. I wondered, vaguely curious, if it was K's blood, or mine.

"Why do I destroy?" he asked.

I said, "Why do I push people to destruction?"

"Because you're a woman," he said.

I said, "Because it's what you do. It's what you've always done. You have a genius for it."

I waited for his reaction. To my surprise, K took the edge of his shirt and wiped the sweat off my face and the tears from his cheeks. Then he smiled and cupped the back of my head—which, speaking from experience, is not unlike getting cuffed by a lion. He said, "Okay, my girl. Get yourself under a mosquito net before you get bitten to death."

WE SLEPT FOR a couple more hours. Before dawn I heard K get up. The screen door on the veranda whined open and slammed shut as he let himself out of the cage. I lay in bed watching the gray dawn turn pink and the lake magic itself into a shiny, flat, rose-colored mirror. Mapenga was up—I heard him talking to the lion as he hurried up from the pavilion to the workshops. Kapenta rigs motored home steadily; I could see their craning necks and long-reaching nets. They evoked a brood of ancient herons. As they pulled up onto the island, I could hear the men who crewed the boats shouting to one another. They were calling out the night's catch in high, singing voices and I envied them.

Mapenga was saying to the lion in a steady, laughing voice, "Mambo Jambo, boy. How's the lion? Mambo, my boy. How's Mambo?"

I got up and lit the stove to make tea. K came back from his early-morning prayer session. He looked, as he often did after being with God, as if his face had been lightly glazed—a sort of peeling shine glowed off his cheeks. He put his arm over my shoulder and asked if I was okay.

"Fine."

Mapenga shouted to me that he'd like some tea, if I was making some anyway. K asked for hot water and honey. I cleared a place from the debris of last night's supper (wineglasses, the remains of a fish skeleton seething with greasy ants). Mambo came to the wire and took a few, halfhearted swipes at the laundry I had hung up over the top of the cage. He needed breakfast.

The routine of tea, the casual domesticity, the drying underwear on the fence, the unfed cat, the two-o'clock-in-the-morning quarrels, the implied apology, the unwashed dishes.

From a distance, whatever this was could easily be mistaken for a marriage.

The Big Silence

The Elders

MUKUMBURA IS WHERE K was stationed when he wasn't on patrol. It was where he came to relax from the war. Once a month he left the bush and came back to Mukumbura to sleep and get drunk and clean his gun and have a shower. And to account for every round fired in the last three weeks.

"Bullets aren't free, man. We need a gook for every round."

Then he was issued with fresh ammunition and three weeks' supply of food and sent back out into the bush with three other men. There, jumpy and cracking, and worn down by the heat and the dirt and the fear and the killing, they shot at everything that moved. Fuck the bullet counter back at HQ.

Mukumbura-by-the-Sea, they called it. But there was no sea. Just a huge, ugly sand dune; a desolate stretch of land that looked as if all the leftovers from the beautiful parts of the country were snipped off and left here in an untidy pile of tailings and scrub. To its north, the silted wasteland sank into a river and thereafter into Mozambique. To the south it roped over rocky knots of land until it stalled in the lush valleys that fell beyond Mount Darwin.

Of all the places we came to follow K's war, this was the most frozen in time. It was as if the war had stepped away from its desk for a moment, but would be right back. Loops of barbed wire ran along high security fences, which snaked and seared through a uniformly blond landscape. A flagpole poked stiffly from the tired tide of sand. Long, low buildings buckled under a flat glare of sun—green and metallic and hot. These crouching saunas were buildings for men without women, men who had no expectation or need of comfort. The old airstrip was still serviceable, not because of any upkeep since the war days but because nothing had had the energy to ruin it. For nearly thirty years, it had baked itself flatter and firmer. A flock of goats helpfully kept its surface nibbled down to a scrub. A torn, white plastic bag jerked and danced across it.

Mukumbura had no border post. It had no expectation that anyone would come here for any good reason, not even to flee into Mozambique. Instead of customs and immigration, then, we had to have our passports and vehicle cleared at a small wooden cabin that declared itself the police station. The policemen had taken stools and benches outside and propped themselves up under a mango tree, where they talked and smoked. Seeing us, one of the policemen reluctantly extracted himself from the conversation and followed us lazily into the cabin.

A handwritten sign above the officer in charge's desk declared good-naturedly, TOGETHER, WE CAN FIGHT CRIME.

Under this was a list of offenses with their corresponding fines:

ASSAULT COMMON—$5000.00
PUBLIC FIGHTING—$5000.00
INSULTING/SCOLDING—$2000.00
GAMBLING—$2000.00
DRIVING CATTLE WITHOUT PERMIT—$5000.00

I pointed to the sign and said to K, "This might get expensive for us."

But K didn't respond.

"Are you sulking?"

"No."

"Looks like it from here." I handed my passport to the policeman and said, "Is there a fine for sulking?"

"Madam?"

"Kutsamwa," I said, pulling the corners of my mouth down and stamping my foot.

The policeman laughed. K glowered.

We drove to Harare in almost total silence. It's a long day's drive any way you look at it. With a man who has taken your sins—real and imagined—and stitched them onto the sackcloth of his own soul, it is endless. A wide, rocky track climbed up and out into Rusambo and Mount Darwin. I stared out the window at the villages that lay flat and breathless on this inhospitable ground, as if they were so used to being leveled—as they were during the war—that they were still flinching with the memory of it.

Then, a few kilometers beyond Mount Darwin, the road was suddenly pulled back from its ill-behaved sprawl. Here it was paved and smooth. And the ground on either side of it heaved into a sigh of teasing, fertile, red earth. This earth hosted rich groves of fruit trees, avenues of pine and eucalyptus, rolling cattle range. And it also cultivated the intense jealousy and bitterness of the land-starved, power-starved, food-starved villagers in the north who had fought violently for this very land and who now, twenty-three years after independence, had suddenly been given it by a rogue government that, having drowned the economy in a stagnant pool of corruption, was in need of their support. It was bittersweet victory—too late and too poisoned by bad politics to be an unequivocal prize.

Now the resettled villagers blinked despondently at us as we drove past. They waved us down and shouted. They needed a lift to town. There was no fuel to run the tractor. No fertilizer, boss! No pesticide! Hunger! The farm laborers, kicked off the farms by the new tenants, waved us down too. They saw the Zambian license plates and shouted, "Job, boss! Job!"

Bindura tore into the heart of Mazoe Valley. Here, a green tongue of hip-high corn sagged, droughted and underfed, on the side of the road. A lake uncurled beneath the foot of a hill and I caught, on the air, the bell song of frogs. It was the cooling part of the afternoon when the air is most crushed and raw with smells. We passed an orange orchard that had stained the air sweet and hopeful. It made me say, "You could just leave me here." It seemed as good a place as any to find a lift into town, or a place to spend the night.

K said nothing.

"Or stop sulking."

"I'm not sulking."

"Okay."

"I'm just . . ." Then nothing.

"Would it make you feel better to leave me here?"

"I can't."

"Why?"

"It's not safe."

"I can look after myself."

K looked out the window. "You really liked him, didn't you?"

"Oh God."

A long silence.

I said, "I can get a bus to Lusaka."

K laughed.

I said, "You know what your bloody problem is? No one has ever talked back to you because they've only had their mouths half open before you've laid them flat. But I'm not a banana field, or your wife, or your servant. You can't tell me what to think or how to feel or what to say or how to grow."

K said, "I don't like you like this. I liked you the way you were before."

"I am the same person."

K shook his head.

"Yes, I am." I lit a cigarette. "I am, like it or not."

THE NEXT MORNING, I took over driving. We hurried west in silence. Three hours into driving I sniffed and hung my head out of the window. "I've been smelling burning rubber," I said. "Can you smell anything?"

K said nothing.

"And look," I said, tapping the instrument panel, "we seem to have used a lot of fuel."

K looked out the window.

"That's odd, don't you think?"

Silence.

I sang, "I talk to the trees, but they won't listen to me."

Nothing.

"*Fergodsake,* man. Speak! Is anyone home?!"

"Hand brake's on," said K.

"What?"

K pointed to the emergency brake. "You've been driving with the brake on."

"Ah-ha. Well that explains a whole lot." I took the emergency brake off and the pickup surged forward. "Look at that. Miracle of engineering."

K looked out of his window again.

"Why didn't you say anything?"

K scowled.

I started to laugh, trying not to, so that the sound welled up in my chest and burst out of my nose. Then I was shaking with laughter and tears were pouring down my cheeks and I couldn't see the road. I pulled over, got out of the car, and I laughed. I laughed until I looked and sounded like St. Medard, until I was gasping for air and clutching my sides. I laughed until I wept. I laughed until K got out of the car. He sniffed at me. Then he smiled and then there was a gradual sound in the back of his throat, like a growl, and suddenly he was laughing too and then the two of us were howling and holding on to the back of the pickup and laughing, our knees weak.

"Come on," he said at last. "I'll drive. You drink beer and tell me what's happening on the side of the road. You're very good at that."

"Okay."

"Peace?"

I wanted to say that I'd never been at war. Instead, "Peace," I agreed.

A great storm was gathering in the west and it tumbled toward us. It towered up over our heads and reached into the tops of trees and when we met it, we were swallowed in a wall of water and energy. The pickup was buffeted and pummeled and it planed unsteadily across the slick surface of the road. Other vehicles—few as they were—were almost invisible, materializing only once they were upon us, like ghostly apparitions. We drove on, shouting to each other over the sounds of the storm—roaring rain and a high, wailing song of wind. I felt strangely exhilarated, liberated, by the rain. It had forced us to roll up our windows. It had forced us—two unlikely souls brought together by a spectacular series of accidents that went back long before we were born—back into that necessary sense of partnership. If nothing else, we had brought each other this far, and now we were obliged to get each other home.

We turned off at Mkuti and wound our way back down to Lake Kariwa, leaving the storm rocking and thundering behind us. At Kariwa, K retrieved his gun from his colleague. Then, instead of heading back to Sole immediately, he started to drive to the top of the town, taking a road that wound around the shantytowns (buildings stitched together from used turbines discarded by Kariwa's hydroelectric project) and through a lush, high-walled suburb until we were on the summit of a cone-shaped hill.

K got out of the car. "I want to show you something."

I climbed out and followed him to the edge of the road.

"Look," he said. He pointed down to one of the houses that lay below us. It was a large white building, sandblasted and white-washed, with a copper roof that gleamed a warm apricot. A vast garden rolled out from beyond the house: a cropped lawn, palm trees, bougainvillea hedges, honeysuckles and creepers cascading golden blooms. A delicious monster plant wrapped itself around a jacaranda tree and a hedge of hibiscus separated a neat vegetable garden that had been fenced in against monkeys. A regiment of poinsettias and snowball bushes lined a meticulous brick driveway. Two gardeners were tending a rock garden, which was speared with aloe and cacti and carpeted with succulents.

K turned and got back into the car and we drove without talking until we reached the Zambian border. It wasn't until we had cleared the border and were driving out of Sitatunga, on the Zambian side of the border, that K said, "I built that whole place myself." He took his hands off the steering wheel to show me his work-worn fingers. "Every brick and nail of that house came from these hands." He looked out the window and I saw his jaw jump. He shook his head. "It's just an elaborate fucking tomb for Luke now. That's all it is."

The road tumbled out of the Kariwa heights and followed the course of the Pepani, down rocky ledges that flapped with peeling paper bark commiphora trees and into the low sink of the valley. Stalls had been set up here at the instigation of aid agencies to promote the manufacture of straw baskets and mats and baobab-bark rugs. It was an attempt to replace the illicit trade in wildlife and gems that had flourished here until recently. I made K stop and I bought laundry baskets for Mum and my sister.

At the Sole Valley turnoff, we swung east and now this place seemed familiar and kind to me. I waved at the policeman at the roadblock and felt friendly toward the bored truckers and bright prostitutes at the corner tavern (OBEY YOU'RE THUST, someone had painted in large black letters across the white veranda wall in our absence). Evening was coming as we turned into the fish farm, and the light had ripened, sweet and filtered. Doves bobbed stiffly over the road, picking at spilt grain and complaining softly that no one cared, no one cared. They'd never care.

At camp, the dogs were waiting at the top of the steps for someone to bring them their supper. The BBC was discussing world cricket scores from a fork in the tamarind tree. Mum was spraying purple medicine on Isabelle the turkey, who had been bitten by one of the little dogs on the right wing. Dad was smoking his pipe, drinking tea, and reading aloud from *Aquaculture Today*.

"Thanks," I said to K.

K nodded.

He helped me carry my bags into the camp and then walked back to the pickup. I followed him. He opened his door, he hung over the top of it, and then he said, "Don't think that I haven't thought about giving up."

"What?" I said.

"Over and over, I've asked myself, who would miss me? Why am I doing this? Who am I doing this for?" He paused. "Then I remember that no one is given a burden too heavy for them to carry. That's why I carry on." K got in the car and started the engine. He said, "I carry on, because I can."

And then he shut the door and he was gone. One lonely white pickup bumping and jolting down a red road in the Sole Valley until it came to the corner where the donkeys were grazing, and there it turned, and was gone from view.

The Journey Is Now

THOSE OF US who grow in war are like clay pots fired in an oven that is overhot. Confusingly shaped liked the rest of humanity, we nevertheless contain fatal cracks that we spend the rest of our lives itching to fill.

All of us with war-scars will endeavor to find some kind of relief from the constant sting of our incompleteness—drugs, love, alcohol, God, death, truth. K and I, each of us cracked in our own way by our participation on the wrong side of the same war, gravitated to each other, sure that the other held a secret balm—the magic glaze—that might make us whole. I thought he held shards of truth. He thought I held love.

Those of us who grow in war know no boundaries. After all, that most sacred and basic boundary of all (Thou shalt not kill) is not only ignored in war, but outright flaunted and scoffed at. Kill! Slot! Scribble! We (guilty and secret and surviving, and more cunning than the dead) will seep into unseen cracks to find solace. And we will do so without thinking twice, since we are without skins, without membranes, without the usual containments of civilization. We know that life is cheap and that the secret to an inner peace is so dear and so elusive as to be almost unattainable.

K and I met and journeyed and clashed like titans. And, at the end of it all, he asked me not to contact him again. Instead of giving each other some kind of peace and understanding, we had inflamed existing wounds. Far from being a story of reconciliation and understanding, this ended up being a story about what happens when you stand on tiptoe and look too hard into your own past and into the things that make us war-wounded the fragile, haunted, powerful men-women that we are. K and I fell headlong—free fall—into terror, love, hate, God, death, burial.

It's more than a body can take.

Then, months after our journey together, as this book was on its way out of my hands, I received the following e-mail from him:

Hi Bo,

It's been a loooong time Precious, but at last i have email. Have laughed off ever trying to get a phone. Tree fell on the last antenna. I asked you not to contact this arse for a few reasons. Number one: that you could write what you wished without you writing to ask for the odd input from the Scribbs. So everything written is yours, not mine. Number two: I needed to sort out my own shit. Number three: To water the compost, and hope a teeny bit of brain popped up. So far, lots of water but only fungus up to now.

Hey you're still Precious and and and . . .

I Hope we see one another. This is my eeeeeemail address now and will down load every week. So if you wish To watch the new T V soap, glue yourself to the computer screen.

As Always
Scribbs

GLOSSARY

A guide to the idiosyncratic mix of slang and languages used in the text.

All of a sardine: all of a sudden
Appy: apprentice

Babalas: hangover (Zulu)
Bally: derived from mild expletive "bloody"
Blallered: hit
Benzi: crazy
Biltong: dried meat similar to beef jerky
Bareka: run
Blerry: derived from mild expletive "bloody"
Bonsella: bonus
Bog: toilet or bathroom
Bog roll: toilet paper
Braai: barbecue

Chaya: hit
Chemering: to cry (from Kuchema [Shona])
China: friend (from china crockery, something precious); see also
    Stone China
Chitenge: piece of cloth or wraparound in Zambia
Cool box: cooler
Cookboy: cook
Curry muncher: East Indian

Dagga: marijuana

Dambo: low-lying area, usually clay soil prone to being very wet in the rains and dry and cracked during the dry season

Deezering: running

Donnering: hit, (from the Afrikaans "donder," meaning thunder)

Dop: drink alcohol

Dopping: drinking alcohol

Flattie: crocodile (from *flatdog*—as in a creature that resembles a flattened dog)

Fodya: tobacco (Shona)

Fossils: slang for old people

Fundi: expert

Goffle: person of mixed blood

Gondie: derogative term for blacks

Goolies: testicles

Gwai: tobacco

Hazeku ndaba: no problem

Henry the Fourth: HIV

Hobo: a lot

Hokoyo: beware (Shona)

Hondo: war (Shona)

Honky: white person

Hu-hoos: slang for insects

Hunering: yelling or shouting

Hunna-hunna: problem, usually long and involved

Huzzes: throws or hurls

Imbwa: dog (Shona)

Indaba: problem, from the Xhosa/Zulu meaning "meeting"

Ingutchini: to go mad; Ingutchini is the name of a mental asylum in Zimbabwe

Jesse scrub, jesse bush: a kind of vegetation characterized by thorny, scrubby shrubs

K: kilometer
K-car: gunship helicopter
Kak: shit
Kapenta: small, sardine like fish
Katundu: luggage
Kudala: far away
Kutsamwa: to sulk (Shona)

Lapa: over there
Lekker: nice (Afrikaans)
Laaities: children (Afrikaans)

Mai we: my mother! (from *amai* [Shona])
Mambo: king (Shona)
Maninge: a lot (Shona)
Mapenga: relating to madness (Shona)
Mawhori: whore
Mbambaira: Shona for "potatoes" but also used as slang for land mines
Moffs: homosexual, short for Moffies
Mopane: a kind of tree found in low-lying areas
Munts: people; also used by whites as derogative term for blacks
Murra: a lot
Mwari: God (Shona)

Nyama: meat or game animal (Shona)

Ooh blicksem: my goodness!
Ous: guys, men

Pamsoro: lift (Shona)
Panga: machete
Pawpaw: papaya
Pawpaw: British person (implies that the British are wimps)
Penga: mad (Shona)

Pie-eyed: drunk

Pom: Prisoner of Mother England or Englishman/woman

Porks: slang for Portuguese

Ptozzie: prostitute

Putzi: the maggot formed when a fly lays its eggs under the skin

Sadza: porridge made from ground maize

Scribble: to kill

Sekuru: grandfather (Shona)

Skop: head (Afrikaans)

Shateen: backcountry

Sjambok: whip

Spazed: mentally impaired, also very concerned, "freaked out"

Sterek: a lot

Stompie: cigarette butt

Stone China: best friend, as in a friend that doesn't move and is
     always by your side

Stonked: killed

Struze fact: from "it's as true as fact"

Sumudza: on top (Shona)

Tatenda: thank you (Shona)

Thrombie: long harangue, from thrombosis

Tsotsis: thieves, rogues (Shona)

Underrods: underwear

Vleis: low, seasonally wet area

Voddies: Vodka

Wagon Burner: East Indian

Wazungu (pl.) mazungu (sing.): white person

Wee wee: literally urine, but here means a wimp

ALEXANDRA FULLER

Don't Let's Go to the Dogs Tonight: An African Childhood

PICADOR

Alexandra Fuller was the daughter of white settlers in 1970s war-torn Rhodesia. *Don't Let's Go to the Dogs Tonight* is a memoir of that time when a schoolgirl was as likely to carry a shotgun as a satchel. Fuller tells a story of civil war, of a quixotic battle against nature and loss, and of her family's unbreakable bond with a continent that came to define, shape, scar and heal them. In wry and sometimes hilarious prose, Fuller looks back with rage and love at an extraordinary family living through extraordinary times.

'A book that deserves to be read for generations'
Guardian

'Like Frank McCourt, Fuller writes with devastating humour and directness about desperate circumstances'
Daily Telegraph

OTHER BOOKS
AVAILABLE FROM PAN MACMILLAN

ALEXANDRA FULLER
DON'T LET'S GO
   TO THE DOGS TONIGHT   0 330 49019 2   £7.99

ALEXANDER FRATER
TALES FROM THE TORRID ZONE   0 330 37529 6   £7.99
CHASING THE MONSOON   0 330 43313 X   £7.99
BEYOND THE BLUE HORIZON   0 330 43312 1   £7.99

NORMAN LEWIS
THE TOMB IN SEVILLE   0 330 43538 8   £7.99

All Pan Macmillan titles can be ordered from our website,
www.panmacmillan.com, or from your local bookshop
and are also available by post from:

Bookpost, PO Box 29, Douglas, Isle of Man IM99 1BQ
Credit cards accepted. For details:
Telephone: 01624 677237
Fax: 01624 670923
E-mail: bookshop@enterprise.net
www.bookpost.co.uk

Free postage and packing in the United Kingdom

Prices shown above were correct at the time of going to press.
Pan Macmillan reserve the right to show new retail prices on covers
which may differ from those previously advertised in the text
or elsewhere.